Empowering Young Black Males

Courtland C. Lee

ERIC Counseling and Personnel Services Clearinghouse
2108 School of Education
The University of Michigan
Ann Arbor, Michigan 48109-1259

ERIC Counseling and Personnel Services Clearinghouse
2108 School of Education
The University of Michigan
Ann Arbor, MI 48109-1259

ISBN 1-56109-042-5

This publication was prepared with partial funding from the Office of
Educational Research and Improvement, U.S. Department of Education
under contract no. RI88062011. The opinions expressed in this report do not
necessarily reflect the positions or policies of OERI, the Department of
Education, or ERIC/CAPS.

A Crème de la Crème
Publication

Awarded to those ERIC/CAPS publications that are based on solid, theoretically sound, conceptual foundations and that have achieved rigorous field validation through the replication of effective programs and practices in a variety of educational settings.

Honor Roll of Crème de la Crème Publications

- *Comprehensive Guidance Programs That Work,* by Norman C. Gysbers and Guidance Program Field Writers
- *Invitational Learning for Counseling and Development,* by William W. Purkey, John J. Schmidt and Contributors
- *The Teacher Advisor Program: An Innovative Approach to School Guidance,* by Robert D. Myrick, Linda S. Myrick and Contributors
- *Learning Styles Counseling,* by Shirley A. Griggs
- *Empowering Young Black Males,* by Courtland C. Lee

This book is dedicated to those Black men who showed me the way.

CONTENTS

INTRODUCTION

Dr. Courtland Lee begins this monograph with the compelling and cogent observation that, "frustration, underachievement and ultimate failure comprise the educational reality for scores of Black male youth." He astutely observes that "...Black males tend to experience massive alienation from the educational process in America's schools." Though "school improvement" and "educational reform" have been key educational goals in the past decade, Dr. Lee suggests that they have done little to affect the situation of young Black males whose "...educational failure makes them an endangered species" and who are "...losing ground at a perilous rate."

While other scholars and researchers have expressed alarm over the plight of the young Black male, and the horrendous price our society has paid and will continue to pay unless we are able to reverse this situation, Dr. Lee is unique in offering a field-validated approach for counselors and teachers that offers hope to young Black males that their school experiences may indeed be changed for the better.

Avoiding slogans and simple solutions, Dr. Lee describes a model for empowering young Black males that presents schools and communities with a viable approach that appropriately enlists the efforts of school counselors, teachers, parents and key community leaders. The focus is on real change—change in how the young Black male perceives himself and the skills he develops; and a change from the predominantly negative experiences imposed on young Black males to a core of positive, developmental experiences that will empower them to cope with a difficult, demanding world. The result is a new sense of hope and motivation for young Black males; it is also an answer to an oft-repeated request of counselors and school staff for a valid approach to empowering young Black males.

I first became aware of Dr. Lee's empowerment model when he spoke at an ERIC/CAPS workshop on implementing comprehensive school guidance programs. His remarks intrigued and excited the audience—here was something more than "just talking" about the problem, something that counselors and school staff could *do*. So I asked him to share his ideas and experiences in a monograph for ERIC/CAPS. He has succeeded wonderfully well! This monograph provides the reader with both a penetrating understanding of the problem, *and* practical interventions for contributing to the empowerment of young Black males.

Our high estimation of the quality of this book has lead us to honor it with inclusion in the Crème de la Crème monograph series—*the best of the best.* We believe that the daunting problems young Black males face deserve the very best efforts we can make to assist them. This inspired monograph by Dr. Courtland Lee will give hope and sound direction to all who are sincere about confronting and overcoming this enormous waste of human potential.

Garry R. Walz
Director, ERIC/CAPS

ABOUT THE AUTHOR

Courtland C. Lee is an associate professor and director of the Counselor Education Program at the University of Virginia. His areas of research specialization include multicultural counseling and adolescent development. He has published numerous articles and book chapters on adolescent development, counseling Black males, and counseling across cultures. He is also the co-editor of a book on multicultural counseling.

Dr. Lee is the former editor of the *Journal of Multicultural Counseling and Development* and serves on the Advisory Board of the *International Journal for the Advancement of Counselling* and the editorial board of the *Journal for Counseling and Development*. He is active in national and international professional organizations and is a Past-President of the Association for Multicultural Counseling and Development. He is also a member of the National Council on African American Men.

A former teacher and school counselor, he has served as a psychoeducational consultant on Black male issues to numerous educational institutions.

ACKNOWLEDGEMENTS

I am indebted to a number of individuals for their assistance with the development of this book. First and foremost are the school counselors throughout the country who have attended my workshops and seminars on counseling young Black males. I am greatly impressed with their dedication and commitment to the cause of Black male youth. These individuals have taken my counseling models back to their schools and implemented them in creative ways. Many of their ideas for improving my empowerment programs are presented in this book. I am grateful for their efforts.

I am deeply grateful to the Richmond, Virginia Public School System for being one of the first school districts to make a system-wide commitment to my Black male empowerment programs. Special thanks must go to Dr. Laverne Spurlock, Director of Guidance and Mr. Aubery Fountain, Counselor at Thomas Jefferson High School for their assistance and encouragement. I am also indebted to the Alexandria, Virginia school system for including me in the planning and implementation of their Black male empowerment efforts. My work with that system was instrumental in helping me shape ideas on educational advocacy for Black male students. A special note of gratitude goes to Ken Firling, Coordinator of Special Programs and Dr. Charles Jackson, Assistant Superintendent for Pupil and Personnel Services for their friendship and support.

I must also express my gratitude to Reverend Calvin Woods and the Brotherhood of Greater Liberty Baptist Church in New Orleans, Louisiana.

My association with the men of Greater Liberty was the impetus for the development of the program to prepare adult Black men for service as role models for male youth. I am grateful for all of their help and inspiration.

I am also indebted to Marian Wright Edelman, founder and president of the Childrens' Defense Fund, who expressed an interest in my ideas on empowering Black males. She personally presented them to schools, churches, and community agencies across the country through the auspices of her organization. I am most appreciative of her efforts on behalf of Black male empowerment.

A special note of gratitude must go to Robyn Nelson Jackson who assisted in the proofreading and editing of the manuscript. Without her able editorial assistance the book would not have been successfully completed.

Finally, I am deeply grateful to my wife, Antoinette, for her love and support. I greatly appreciate having had the benefit of her experiences and insights in the development of this book.

Courtland C. Lee

PREFACE

Black males in contemporary American society face major challenges to their psychological and social development. Social and economic indicators of Black male development in the United States provide a profile of an individual whose quality of life is in serious jeopardy. From an early age, it has become increasingly apparent that Black males are confronted with a series of obstacles in their attempts to attain academic, career, and personal-social success.

Social and economic indicators of Black male development in the United States provide a profile of an individual whose quality of life is in serious jeopardy.

Achieving manhood has historically been a complex and challenging task for the Black male in America. Therefore, Black manhood must be carefully fostered from an early age by major socializing agents and institutions. Parents and the family represent the most important socializing agents and institution for young males. However, the school plays a significant role as a socializing institution for young Black males. Within the school, counseling professionals can play a major role in promoting the development of young Black males.

Within the school, counseling professionals can play a major role in promoting the development of young Black males.

The purpose of this book is to provide school counselors and related mental health professionals with important information to help them address the crisis of the Black male. The focus of the book is on Black male educational empowerment and how pupil personnel professionals can promote it in the school setting. The book examines important issues in the development of young Black males that must be understood to effectively facilitate their educational and social empowerment. In addition, it provides direction for implementing intervention programs that promote Black male empowerment in elementary and secondary schools. The book also suggests ways to actively involve teachers and the inherent strengths of Black communities in this important process.

Chapter 1 offers an overview and interpretation of current statistical data on Black male educational progress from grades K–12. Chapter 2 is an examination of the early psychosocial development of Black males: Historical and environmental impediments to childhood and adolescent Black male development are examined. A discussion of Black culture and its role in the development of Black male youth is presented in Chapter 3. Chapter 4 is comprised of four Empowerment Training Modules. Module 1 is an examination of an educational empowerment program for promoting optimal academic achievement and positive social behavior among Black males at the elementary school level. An empowerment intervention for promoting manhood among Black males in grades 7–12 is presented in Module 2. In Module 3, a guide for getting men from Black communities involved in educational empowerment efforts with young boys is offered. Module 4 focuses on educational advocacy for Black male youth. It provides direction for counselor consultation to help teachers and other educators understand the dynamics of Black male development. A curriculum for a professional development experience for school personnel on understanding Black males and promoting their academic success is presented. Chapter 5 is a call to action for school counselors and related professionals that presents a comprehensive plan for the empowerment of young Black males.

This book is designed as an action manual for school counseling professionals. The concepts and programs presented here are designed to guide counseling practice for promoting the academic, career, and personal-social empowerment of young Black males.

This book is designed as an action manual for school counseling professionals. The concepts and programs presented here are designed to guide counseling practice for promoting the academic, career, and personal-social empowerment of young Black males. It is hoped that the awareness and knowledge gained as well as the skills developed from this book will make counselors a part of the solution, rather than a part of the problem.

CHAPTER 1

The Black Male in America's Schools: A Troubled Profile

Overview

Education is power. It is a lifelong process of developing the knowledge and skills to be all that one can be. Education is also a highly prized commodity. In most cultural groups it is considered to be the primary vehicle for improving the quality of life. Black people in America, for example, have always placed a great value on education. Indeed, the social and economic progress that Blacks have made in this country has been in direct proportion to the educational opportunities available to them.

Black males in contemporary American society, however, face formidable challenges to their educational development. There is a serious stifling of achievement, aspiration, and pride on the part of many Black males in school systems throughout the country. Frustration, underachievement, and ultimate failure comprise the educational reality for scores of Black male youth.

This chapter presents an examination of data related to the school enrollment and performance of Black males. In addition, a discussion of the implications in the data for counselor action is provided.

Education is...a highly prized commodity. In most cultural groups it is considered to be the primary vehicle for improving the quality of life.

Frustration, underachievement, and ultimate failure comprise the educational reality for scores of Black male youth.

1

Profile in Failure

Data on the educational attainment of Black male youth from a variety of sources (House of Representatives, 1990; Jones, 1986; House of Representatives, 1991; National Black Child Development Institute, 1990; Reed, 1988; House of Representatives, 1989) present a troubled profile. To illustrate:

Black males are far more likely than other ethnic/gender groups to be placed in general education and vocational high school curricular tracks than in an academic track.

- Black males are far more likely than other ethnic/gender groups to be placed in general education and vocational high school curricular tracks than in an academic track.
- Black males are three times more likely to be placed in classes for the educable mentally retarded and for students with learning disabilities than in gifted and talented classes.
- Black males drop out or are pushed out of school systems at higher rates than other ethnic/gender groups.
- Black males are suspended from school more frequently and for longer periods of time than other ethnic/gender groups.
- Black males complete high school at significantly lower rates than other ethnic/gender groups.
- Between 1976 and 1986 despite increases in overall minority enrollment, including Black female enrollment, college enrollment rates of Black males 18–24 declined from 35% to 28%.

What is evident from this profile is that Black males tend to experience massive alienation from the educational process in America's schools.

What is evident from this profile is that Black males tend to experience massive alienation from the educational process in America's schools. Significantly, a recent report prepared by a committee to study the status of the Black in the New Orleans Public Schools graphically underscores these data. Though Black males represented 43% of the public school population in that city during the 1986–87 academic year, they accounted for 58% of the non-promotions, 65% of the suspensions, 80% of the expulsions, and 45% of the dropouts (Committee to Study the Status of the Black Male in the New Orleans Public Schools, 1988).

This report from the New Orleans Public Schools is by no means an anomaly. Indications of massive academic failure on the part of Black males can be found in school systems across the country. Such failure often begins as early as the third grade, with many Black males either dropping out or being pushed out of school for behavioral problems by the seventh grade.

Such data and reports are compounded by the fact that Black males are frequently the victims of negative attitudes and lowered expectations from teachers, counselors, and administrators. Educators may expect to encounter academic and social problems from Black males, which often lead to a self-fulfilling prophecy (Washington & Lee, 1982). The recipients of lowered expectations from teachers, counselors, and administrators, Black males experience alienation in school, making failure an integral part of their educational experience.

Importantly, efforts are under way to improve the educational development of Black males. Freiberg (1991), for example, reports on proposals around the country to separate Black male youth into schools or classes where the emphasis will be on raising their self-respect, promoting racial and cultural pride, and overcoming obstacles to their educational success. A growing number of school systems have implemented or are considering segregated educational experiences for Black males. However, these proposals are very controversial and have provoked fierce debate among educators and scholars.

It is apparent that Black males face major hurdles in striving for academic and social success. While many Black males achieve significant educational

Indications of massive academic failure on the part of Black males can be found in school systems across the country. Such failure often begins as early as the third grade....

...Black males experience alienation in school, making failure an integral part of their educational experience.

A growing number of school systems have implemented or are considering segregated educational experiences for Black males.

success, many others experience major challenges, often becoming frustrated, losing hope, and ultimately dropping out or being pushed out of school. The consequences of this are significant limitations on socioeconomic mobility, ultimately leading to high rates of unemployment, crime, and incarceration for growing numbers of young Black men. Indeed, figures related to declining participation in the labor force, increasing crime rates, and incarceration for Black men (Cordes, 1985; Gary, 1981; Gibbs, 1988a; McGhee, 1984) suggest that these consequences of educational failure make them an endangered species (Gibbs, 1984; Leavy, 1983).

Indeed, figures related to declining participation in the labor force, increasing crime rates, and incarceration for Black men... suggest that these consequences of educational failure make them an endangered species....

Black males are losing ground at a perilous rate.

Meeting the Challenge: Implications for Counselors

At a time when rapidly changing technology requires a skilled and well educated workforce, Black males are losing ground at a perilous rate. The situation calls for aggressive steps to be taken by educators. They are faced with the challenge of insuring that Black males are provided educational opportunities that will maximize their potential. For this reason, it is important that counseling professionals play a major role in offering solutions to the educational problems of Black male youth. Concerted efforts are needed to develop comprehensive approaches for facilitating the academic, career, and personal-social empowerment of young Black males. Such approaches should reflect the needs and realities of Black male students. The remainder of this book examines specific counselor functions considered necessary for empowering young Black males for optimal educational achievement. It also explores important concepts that counselors must understand and appreciate if they are to be effective agents of empowerment for Black male youth.

CHAPTER 2

The Psychosocial Development of Young Black Males: Issues and Impediments

Introduction

Successful implementation of school-based empowerment experiences for young Black males must be predicated on an understanding of the dynamics associated with childhood and adolescent psychosocial development from a Black male perspective. This chapter provides an overview of important historical and social issues that must be considered in the psychosocial development of young Black males.

Key Developmental Issues of Childhood and Adolescence

Theorists and researchers have suggested that major aspects of human development unfold in a series of life stages and are influenced by both heredity and environment (Erikson, 1950; Havighurst, 1972; Kohlberg, 1966; Piaget, 1970). As individuals progress through the life stages, they must master a series of developmental tasks. Mastery of tasks at one stage of life influences success with those in succeeding stages. Conversely, failure to master developmental tasks at one stage can negatively influence success in later stages.

...major aspects of human development unfold in a series of life stages and are influenced by both heredity and environment.

5

Childhood is the period in life when an individual must develop a sense of trust, autonomy, initiative, and industry.

Erikson (1950), for example, succinctly conceptualized the developmental stages and tasks of childhood and adolescence. Childhood is the period in life when an individual must develop a sense of trust, autonomy, initiative, and industry. These dimensions can be seen in such things as a child learning to relate emotionally to parents and siblings, learning to walk and talk, developing a self-concept, and learning to read and write.

Adolescence follows. This is the period when an individual begins the important life transition from childhood to adulthood. It is during this span of time that a child should develop a sense of identity observable in events such as learning gender-appropriate social roles and behaviors, achieving emotional independence from significant adults, and setting educational and career goals.

...for Black males in America, successfully completing these early developmental stages and tasks has often been problematic....

It is important to note that for Black males in America, successfully completing these early developmental stages and tasks has often been problematic due to a complex set of historical and social factors. In many instances, these factors interact to prevent Black males from mastering crucial developmental tasks in childhood and adolescence. In turn, this significant lack of mastery negatively influences their academic, career, and social success in the later stages of life.

Impediments to the Psychosocial Development of Black Males

From an historical perspective, manhood has not been a birthright for Black males....

From an historical perspective, manhood has not been a birthright for Black males (Hernton, 1965; Lee, 1990; Staples, 1978). They have not generally been granted traditional masculine privilege or power in the United States. Social, cultural, and economic forces throughout American history have combined to keep Black males from assuming accepted masculine roles (Staples, 1983; Wilkinson & Taylor, 1977). The White male, from boyhood, is generally socialized with a masculine sensibility comprised of an awareness that power and control are his birthright, as well as the primary means of insuring personal respect, financial security, and success (Goldberg, 1976; Pleck & Sawyer, 1974).

The Black male, on the other hand, has often been denied such possibilities of manhood. This denial process has been an integral part of the dynamics of oppression and racism that have pervaded the Black experience in America (Grier & Cobbs, 1968; Thomas & Sillen, 1972). Beginning with the slavery experience, the Black male has been an object of fear (Grier & Cobbs, 1968; Hilliard, 1985; Staples, 1978). The Black man, and his implied physical prowess and leadership ability, has been perceived as representing the greatest threat to the social order. Therefore, the power structure within American society has insured that Black males have had limited access to the traditional sex role values and behaviors associated with power, control, status, and achievement. Throughout American history, the power structure has initiated various social and economic actions that have resulted in the subordination of the Black male and the cancellation of his masculine advantage in the larger society (Staples, 1978; Taylor, 1977). The inability in many cases to attain masculine roles has kept many Black men from realizing even the most basic aspects of masculine privilege and power, namely life-sustaining employment and the ability to support a family (Staples, 1978).

The persistence of barriers to the achievement and expression of manhood has generally resulted in significant social disadvantage for Black males. Such disadvantage has been a major contributor to the failure, in many instances, to master crucial developmental tasks in childhood and adolescence. In a

The White male, from boyhood, is generally socialized with a masculine sensibility comprised of an awareness that power and control are his birthright....

The Black man, and his implied physical prowess and leadership ability, has been perceived as representing the greatest threat to the social order.

The persistence of barriers to the achievement and expression of manhood has generally resulted in significant social disadvantage for Black males.

society that historically has not acknowledged manhood as a birthright for Black males, achieving optimal psychosocial development has been difficult for Black male youth.

It is not uncommon to find environmental forces converging to impact negatively on the psychosocial development of scores of Black males in contemporary society. They are often confronted with extreme environmental stress during the crucial early years of life (Hilliard, 1985; Myers & King, 1980). This stress is manifested in home, community, and school experiences. For example, a majority of Black boys, particularly in urban areas, are born into home and community environments characterized by traditions of poverty, crime, unemployment, inequitable educational opportunities, and a perceived sense of social and cultural alienation among many men. Young boys nurtured in such environments may experience difficulty in developing the basic trust, sense of autonomy, initiative, and industry which characterize the developmental tasks of the childhood years.

Successful completion of these developmental tasks can be further hampered by school experiences distinguished by ineffective teaching strategies, as well as predetermined negative views on Black males and their learning potential on the part of educators (Washington & Lee, 1982). Rather than developing a sense of industry that comes with mastering fundamental skills in reading, writing, and computing during the all-important elementary school years, many young Black male students experience a sense of frustration with the teaching-learning process, which lays the groundwork for future academic and social failure.

It is not unusual, therefore, for Black males to reach adolescence with a basic mistrust of their environment, doubts about their abilities, and confusion about their place in the social structure. This makes developing an identity during the crucial boyhood-to-manhood transition of the adolescent years extremely

Black males...are often confronted with extreme environmental stress during the crucial early years of life....

It is not unusual...for Black males to reach adolescence with a basic mistrust of their environment....

problematic. Compounding this problem is the social reality that Black boys may have to engage in the process of identity formation with minimal or no positive adult male role modeling. Significantly, identity-formation during adolescence is a process in which youth develop aspects of their personal and social identities by selecting and identifying with various role models. Given the historical social and economic limitations placed on Black manhood in America, the range of Black adult male role models available to adolescent boys may often be severely restricted. The developmental passage to adulthood becomes a confusing experience for many Black male youth because the evolution of gender-appropriate roles and behaviors for Black men has often been stifled by historical and social powerlessness.

...the range of Black adult male role models available to adolescent boys may often be severely restricted.

By the age of 18, the sum total of these impediments to psychosocial development in childhood and adolescence can often be seen in negative and self-destructive attitudes, behaviors, and values among young Black males. The impact of such factors has resulted in the direct negative consequences of educational underachievement, unemployment, delinquency, substance abuse, homicide, and incarceration in disproportionate numbers for Black male youth (Cordes, 1985; Gibbs, 1988a).

Conclusion

While scores of Black male youth develop the survival strategies, coping mechanisms, and forms of resistance to successfully master the developmental tasks of childhood and adolescence, it must be understood that social and environmental forces have historically been stacked against psychosocial development for Black males. For this reason, counselors committed to the empowerment of Black male youth must first understand the dimensions of their psychosocial development. It is important to appreciate that

...counselors committed to the empowerment of Black male youth must first understand the dimensions of their psychosocial development.

these dimensions are complex and challenging in a society that has historically placed Black men at social and economic risk.

CHAPTER 3

Black Culture: Its Role in the Development of Black Male Youth

Introduction

Any discipline that would seek to understand the development of Black male youth must consider the cultural dynamics which shape that development. Empowerment strategies should be predicated on an understanding of Black culture and its crucial role in fostering development. Black educators and psychologists have concluded that there are aspects of the Black cultural experience in America that have evolved out of African tradition which have a significant relationship with mental health and psychosocial development (Cross, 1974; Harper, 1973; Nobles, 1972; Pasteur & Toldson, 1982; White, 1970). These conclusions have led to a framework for understanding Black behavior and personality.

An examination of core Black culture (i.e., the attitudes, behaviors, and values which have developed in relatively homogeneous Black communities where rudimentary Afrocentric ways of life have been preserved to a great extent), will reveal that Americans of African descent have developed a world-view that reflects the historical experience of Black people in America and is based on African-oriented philosophical assumptions. This world-view encompasses a cultural tradition reflected in the

Empowerment strategies should be predicated on an understanding of Black culture and its crucial role in fostering development.

Americans of African descent have developed a world-view that reflects the historical experience of Black people in America and is based on African-oriented philosophical assumptions.

11

Black expressiveness can be found in the expressive behaviors and cultural life of people world-wide who trace their roots to Africa.

Black expressiveness ...when it has been considered in a traditional European, European American psychoeducational context...has often been viewed as deviant, deficient, or pathological.

concept of **Black expressiveness** (Pasteur & Toldson, 1982). Black expressiveness can be found in the expressive behaviors and cultural life of people world-wide who trace their roots to Africa.

For Black Americans, this concept can be considered the vestigial remains of an African personality distilled through the American experience.

Five important dimensions characterize Black expressiveness. Each of these contribute significantly to Black mental health and psychosocial development. These dimensions represent a healthy fusion of the cognitive, affective, and behavioral aspects of personality. First, Black expressiveness is characterized by a high degree of emotional energy exhibited in interpersonal interactions and behavior. Second, it is marked by a propensity among Black people to exhibit real, honest, and authentic behavior in all human relationships. Third, style and flair are hallmarks of this phenomenon. This is often seen in the creative manner Black people have found to put their personalities on display. Fourth, it is seen in the language and speech traditions of Black people, which are direct, creative, and communicate both information and significant affect. Finally, it is characterized by expressive movement. This is an ability to integrate thought, feeling, and movement into a whole and respond to the environment in a spontaneous fashion.

Collectively, these five dimensions represent the healthy manifestation of Black personality. Black expressiveness is a healthy psychosocial construct and the basis of positive attitudes, values, and behavior. However, when it has been considered in a traditional European, European American psychoeducational context, it has often been viewed as deviant, deficient, or pathological.

Black Culture and Male Socialization

The cultural traditions inherent in Black expressiveness are the foundation of Black male socialization. From an early age, Black boys are socialized into these cultural traditions in the home and larger Black community (Allen, 1981; Staples, 1983; Wilson, 1987). These socializing agents transmit the traditions that comprise the world-view of Black male youth.

A synthesis of this cultural tradition is readily apparent in the personality dynamics of Black males from an early age. It can be considered the basis of a distinct Black male culture (Hale, 1982; Kunjufu, 1986; Majors, 1986). Majors (1986) refers to these personality dynamics as "cool pose" and considers them to be the cornerstone of Black male identity. Observing Black male youth, these dynamics become apparent in the following ways:

The cultural traditions inherent in Black expressiveness are the foundation of Black male socialization. From an early age, Black boys are socialized into these cultural traditions in the home and larger Black community....

Social Behavior

There is a dynamism associated with social behavior of young Black males. Their peer group interactions, for example, are often characterized by high levels of energy. These interactions tend to be very physical and demonstrative. "Woofing" (engaging in aggressive verbal interchanges) or roughhousing with each other, young Black males use their bodies in expressive ways, such as cultivating distinctive handshakes.

In settings where limits are set on behavioral expressiveness, such as school, the cultural dynamism of Black males is often difficult to hold in check for extended periods of time. Young Black males need to physically respond to intellectual, affective, or behavioral stimuli.

...young Black males use their bodies in expressive ways, such as cultivating distinctive handshakes.

Authenticity

A propensity exists among young Black males to exhibit real, honest, and authentic behavior in all interactions.

A propensity exists among young Black males to exhibit real, honest, and authentic behavior in all interactions. This is seen as "being for real" or "telling it like it is." They tend not to stifle their true thoughts, feelings, or behaviors in most social situations. While such authenticity may not always be appreciated or understood by others, Black males tend to cut to the heart of a matter with their genuineness.

Language and Speech

...expressive linguistic traditions are used in order to diffuse tension between young males that could lead to physical aggression.

The language and speech of young Black males is highly expressive and exhibits considerable creativity. Colorful slang expressions, "woofing," playing the "dozens," and the popular "rap" vernacular are innovative ways that have been developed to communicate both the trivial and the profound. Often these expressive linguistic traditions are used in order to diffuse tension between young males that could lead to physical aggression. For example, the oftentimes harsh verbal volleying that accompanies "woofing," can prevent two Black males from coming to physical blows.

Style

Young Black males find creative ways to put their personalities on display.

Young Black males find creative ways to put their personalities on display. One has only to examine the style and flair exhibited by Black males on the basketball court, the swagger associated with walking, hats worn at a jaunty angle, fancy sneakers, or flashy articles of clothing to appreciate the expressiveness inherent in the style of young Black males. These artifacts are attempts to strike a "cool pose" and make a proud statement about oneself.

These personality dynamics are healthy manifestations of Black culture on the part of young Black males. As Majors (1986) suggests, they have also been an important coping mechanism. Rather than confront the traditions of racism and oppression which characterize the Black experience in America with anger and frustration, Black males have released their tension by channeling energies into the development of expressive personality dynamics. Therefore, such dynamics significantly contribute to Black male survival.

Black Male Culture and the School Setting

While many of the expressive dimensions discussed above may be characteristic of young Black females, as well as youth from other ethnic backgrounds, their manifestation among Black males has generally been the most misunderstood in the American social arena. In the school setting, for example, it is not unusual for the dimensions of Black male culture to be seen as a major threat to the established social order. It has been asserted that educators have predetermined negative views concerning Black male culture and may expect to encounter difficulties in their inter- actions with Black male students because of them (Washington & Lee, 1982). These views and the actions educators take related to them are a major reason why scores of young Black males end up mislabeled or negatively tracked in the educational system. Engaging in normal, healthy Black male behavior in school, therefore, can often have negative consequences for male youth.

Counselors and Black Culture: New Perspective on Male Empowerment

A new perspective on Black male empowerment is needed. Empowerment interventions for Black male youth must be implemented with the knowledge that

Black males have released their tension by channeling energies into the development of expressive personality dynamics.

In the school setting...it is not unusual for the dimensions of Black male culture to be seen as a major threat to the established social order.

A new perspective on Black male empowerment is needed.

Counseling professionals must be armed with a solid Black cultural knowledge base to address the educational challenges facing Black males.

Black culture fosters attitudes, behaviors, and values that are positive and promote the development of young males in this culture. Empowerment interventions, therefore, must be undertaken from a perspective that focuses on the development of male youth by promoting Black cultural expressiveness. Counseling professionals must be armed with a solid Black cultural knowledge base to address the educational challenges facing Black males.

CHAPTER 4

Empowerment Training Modules

Chapter 4 is dedicated to four powerful modules which provide the user with specific preparation on how to intervene to empower young Black males. They range in scope from an empowerment program for Black males in grades 3–6 to using the power of elders and employing educational advocacy. Each module provides specific instructions for the user as well as a body of highly useful multi-media resources. The reader is encouraged to examine the modules thoroughly and to commit him or herself to infusing them into the counseling and/or teaching of young Black males. The outcomes can be very rewarding.

MODULE 1

The Young Lions:
An Educational Empowerment Program for Black Males in Grades 3–6

Introduction

Ronald

Ronald is a nine-year-old Black male in the fourth grade at a public elementary school. He comes to school every day proudly wearing the latest fashions including a cap and expensive sneakers with the laces untied. Most days when he comes into the classroom, his female teacher confronts him about removing his cap and tying his shoelaces. Ronald usually storms over to the other side of the room, mumbles under his breath, and grudgingly removes his cap.

As the morning's instruction proceeds, Ronald occupies his time interacting with the other boys who sit around him. He enjoys talking with them, giving them "high fives," and generally joking and teasing with them. The teacher perceives Ronald to be inattentive and the instigator of most of this activity. She proceeds to reprimand him about his behavior.

When the teacher reprimands Ronald, he gets upset at her protestations, claiming that she is picking on him. She claims that he is not paying attention. However, when she presses him about the topic under class discussion, he is able to respond correctly. In fact, Ronald claims that he has raised his hand several times that morning, but that the teacher ignores him.

The teacher notices again that Ronald's shoelaces are still untied. She sternly orders him to tie the laces. Ronald staunchly refuses, stating that this is the way they are supposed to be worn. She states that in her classroom, shoelaces will be tied. Again, she orders him to lace the shoes and moves toward Ronald, placing her hand on his shoulder and looking him squarely in the face.

At this point, Ronald jerks away from the teacher and shouts, "Don't be touchin' me Bitch!" He forcefully walks away from the teacher, picks up a book, and flings it across the classroom. The teacher then orders Ronald to go to the principal's office.

The issues in Ronald's case are representative of those confronting many Black boys in contemporary elementary schools. It must be understood that elementary education in this country is an enterprise greatly influenced by White middle-class female culture. The teaching-learning process at this educational level overwhelmingly represents aspects of this culture. The early years of school for young Black males, therefore, are often characterized by dissimilarity and imbalance. Confronted daily with attitudes, behaviors, and values of teachers, who in many instances are unaware of or insensitive to the personality and behavioral dynamics of Black male culture, bright and capable boys such as Ronald can become alienated from the educational process at an early age (Patton, 1981). A review of this case makes it is easy to speculate that after a number of punitive visits to the principal's office, precipitated by the clash of teacher-student cultural realities, Ronald will be negatively labeled and ultimately consigned to a failure track.

A committed counselor could work to prevent alienation on Ronald's part with programmed intervention at several levels. For example, Module 2 gives direction for consulting with teachers to increase their awareness, knowledge, and skills for successfully teaching Black males. This module, however, presents an intervention program for promoting educational empowerment among Black males at the elementary level, specifically grades 3–6. It is designed to be initiated at third grade level because evidence suggests that educational and social problems for Black children begin to manifest themselves by this time (Morgan, 1980).

Background for the Program

Educators have long stressed the importance of Black consciousness or self-identity to the psychosocial development of Black children (Barnes,

1991; Clark & Clark, 1947; White & Johnson, 1980). Within this context, efforts have been undertaken, in both teaching and counseling, to develop a curriculum that promotes the self-concept of Black children by emphasizing African/African American culture and history (Hale, 1982; Kunjufu, 1984; Lee, 1989; Lee & Lindsey, 1985). Kunjufu (1986) proposes a conceptual framework for developing a relevant counseling curriculum for Black boys that incorporates African/African American culture. He advocates initiating intervention models which encompass the spirit and intent of traditional programs, such as the Boy Scouts and Big Brothers, for the protection and development of young Black males. The objectives of such models should include skill development, Black history, male socialization, recreation, and adult male role models. Kunjufu has identified the Swahili word "Simba," which means "Young Lion," as a generic name for such programs. This chapter describes a program developed, using Kunjufu's proposed framework, as an educational empowerment experience that can be included as part of an elementary school counseling curriculum.

The Program

The program is called "The Young Lions" and is a multisession educational empowerment experience coordinated by counseling professionals for Black boys in grades 3–6. It provides the opportunity for participants to spend quality educational time during the school day with an older Black male who serves as a role model/mentor. The program stresses the development of the motivation and skills necessary for academic success, the development of positive and responsible social behavior, an understanding and appreciation of Black history and culture, and the modeling of positive Black male images.

While an experience such as this would be beneficial for most Black boys in grades 3–6, efforts should be made to insure that those who are experiencing significant academic and/or social frustration in the classroom, such as Ronald in the above case study, are given priority. A major goal of the program is to help boys labeled "at-risk" avoid those problems which often lead to their ultimate failure in school.

Prior to the start of such a program, counselors should be prepared to discuss with parents and school officials the rationale for conducting an educational experience segregated by ethnicity and gender in the school setting. An important argument for conducting such an experience is that it is not unusual for Black boys to be segregated in the school setting, usually for special education classes or for disciplinary reasons. Often the number of Black boys segregated for such purposes is disproportionate to their numbers in the total school population. Therefore, segregating Black boys for an experience such as this, which is proactive and developmental, should be welcomed as a way to promote academic success and decrease disciplinary involvement.

If such a program is to be successful, counselors must include competent Black men as role models/mentors. This is important because of the paucity of Black male educators in elementary schools. These role models/mentors and their interactions with the boys, therefore, must be the cornerstone of the program. Module 3 provides guidelines for getting concerned Black men involved in such a program.

An important feature of the experience is the use of selected Black art forms. Specifically these include music, poetry, folklore, and culture-specific curriculum materials used as educational aids. It has been suggested that such curriculum materials and aesthetic dimensions be incorporated into counseling interventions with Black students as a way to facilitate personal and social growth (Lee & Lindsey, 1985; Lee, 1989; Pasteur & Toldson, 1982).

The program is presented here as a year-long experience. It may however be shortened and intensified according to individual preferences and institutional considerations. The general framework of the program is to assign each boy a role model/mentor for approximately one hour twice a week. Depending upon the number of male volunteers, however, it may be necessary to have a role model/mentor work with more than one boy at a time. In such cases, attempts should be made to keep the student-role model/mentor ratio at 2 to 1. The one-hour sessions should be devoted to working on homework assignments, improving reading and mathematics skills, and discussing personal-social concerns.

The role model/mentors should be responsible for maintaining contact with classroom teachers to ensure a degree of congruity between program activities and classroom learning experiences. In addition, they should make periodic contact with parents regarding the boys' progress in the program.

Twice a month all role models/mentors and their students should gather together in a one-hour session for academic and social-enrichment activities. These activities should focus on self-concept enhancement and the improvement of academic and social behavior. The facilitation of this large group experience should be shared by the role models/mentors.

After a description of the orientation session that launches the entire program, the general purpose, methods of facilitation, and intended educational experiences for these large group sessions are examined in this chapter.

■

The Young Lions: A Gathering of the Pride

Goal of the Program

The goal of this program is to help Black boys in grades 3–6 develop motivation and skills for academic success, positive and responsible social behavior, and an understanding and appreciation of Black culture and history. This is accomplished by providing the opportunity for boys to spend quality educational time during the school day with an older Black male who serves as a role model/mentor. The role model/mentor provides modeling of positive Black male attitudes, behaviors, and values.

Program Orientation

Goal

This session will orient participants to the program, introduce the role models/mentors, and pair up men and boys.

Methods of Facilitation

1. Explain to the boys the purpose and nature of the program: They will work with a role model/mentor for one hour twice a week on homework assignments, reading and mathematics skills, and personal-social issues. Twice a month, they will gather in a large group session for social-enrichment activities. It is important to

emphasize to the boys that to be chosen for participation in the program is an **honor.**

2. Introduce the role models/mentors and explain their role. Stress that these men bring much wisdom and knowledge and are to be considered as "respected elders." As such, they are to be treated with honor and respect.

3. Have each boy introduce himself to the group.

4. Discuss the importance of the name of the program: "The Young Lions." Explain the notion of the lion as "king of the animals" and its traditional importance to African people as a symbol of strength and courage. Introduce the notion that this program will help them to develop the strength and courage of young lions through achieving school success. Tell them that when they gather together as a group they will be referred to as a "pride," which is a company of lions. Their group meetings, therefore, will be referred to as "a gathering of the pride."

5. Make student-role model/mentor assignments. Allow time for participants and their role model/mentor to get acquainted.

Note: After this session, participants begin twice-a-week, one-on-one or small group educational enhancement sessions with role models/ mentors. The next sections describe the bi-monthly communal gatherings of all participants and role models/mentors.

Session 1: Pride

Goal

The goal of this session is to provide participants with an opportunity to enhance their self-esteem.

Methods of Facilitation

1. Find a picture of a pride of lions to put on the door of the meeting room with the message: "Do Not Disturb: Young Lions in Session." (Use this whenever the group meets.)

2. Ask participants to share impressions of lions they have seen on television, in motion pictures, at the zoo, etc. Record impressions on chalkboard. Reiterate to participants that a company of lions is called a "pride." Explain that the word pride also has another important meaning. Conduct the "What is Pride?" exercise (Appendix B). Write the meaning of the word "pride" on the board, "delight or elation arising from some act, possession, or relationship" (definition from Webster's dictionary). Have participants read this meaning out loud. Translate the definition into terms that can be readily understood by the group.

Questions for Group Discussion

a. How many of you have pride?
b. What do you have pride in?
c. What is "Black Pride?"
d. What kinds of things can you do in school to develop pride in yourself?

Intended Educational Experiences

1. To help participants begin increasing their self-esteem.
2. To continue developing a sense of brotherhood among men and boys.
3. To have participants begin to develop a sense of personal pride.

Session 2: When I Grow Up

Goal

The goal of this session is to explore future goals and expectations and what it will take to realize them.

Methods of Facilitation

1. Introduce the concept of the 21st Century. Explain to the group the significance of the start of a new century. Stress the fact that they will be young men in the 21st century.

Questions for Group Discussion

a. How old will you be in the year 2010, 2020, 2030, etc.?
b. Where do you think you will be living in those years? Will you be married? Will you have children?
c. What kind of job will you have?
d. How can doing well in school now help you when you are grown up in the twenty-first century?
e. What things that you are learning in school now will help you in the 21st century?

Intended Educational Experiences

1. To have participants begin focused thinking about their futures.
2. To impress upon group members the relationship between present academic achievement and future goals.

Sessions 3–5: Bad Times

Goals

The goals of these sessions are: (1) to have boys critically examine the dynamics of the academic and social problems confronting them as students and (2) to have them develop proactive strategies and techniques for confronting these challenges.

Methods of Facilitation

1. Play the recording, "Bad Times," by the group Tavares. In conjunction with the lyrics of this song, develop a series of situations for participants to role play that involve problems they face in the school setting: for example, role plays involving confrontations with teachers. Using these role plays, help the boys develop strategies for dealing effectively with these problems.

Questions for Group Discussion

a. What are some problems that you have in school? Why do you think you have these problems?
b. Do you feel that you are treated differently from the Black girls or the White children in school?
c. Most of the time, when you get into trouble at school, is it your fault or do you think that the teachers are just picking on you?
d. What can you learn from having bad times at school?
e. What can you do to keep from having bad times at school?

2. Have participants read aloud the poem "Mother to Son" by Langston Hughes (Appendix A). This poem is a mother's exhortation to her son not to give up because he experiences bad times and hardship in life. Explain the poem's message and discuss it with the participants.

Intended Educational Experiences

1. To help boys develop awareness, knowledge, and skills in problem-identification and constructive problem-solving.
2. To help participants gain an appreciation of Black male struggle and persistence.

Session 6: Game Day**

(** A session such as this could be repeated throughout the program.)

Goal

The goal of this session is to increase the level of sportsmanship and constructive physical activity among participants.

Method of Facilitation

Engage in some form of physical activity. For example, organize a group basketball game: boys vs. men. Discuss with the group why it is important to have a strong body, as well as a strong mind.

Intended Educational Experiences

1. To have participants become aware of the importance of physical fitness and its relationship to success.
2. To enhance the sense of community among boys and men by having them interact outside of an educational context.

---------------■---------------

Sessions 7–9: Heroes

Part 1: "Great Kings of Africa"

Goal

The goal of these sessions is to have participants gain a greater appreciation for and understanding of the accomplishments of their African forefathers.

Methods of Facilitation

1. Play the recording, "Waaslu," by Olatunji or similar African music and ask boys about their impressions of Africa.
2. Explore with the group the following questions: How many of you have ever thought that your ancestors could have been kings? What is a king? What does a king do?
3. From encyclopedias and resources on Africa (e.g., "Great Kings of Africa" series from Anheuser-Busch, Inc.), prepare information on great African kings to share and discuss with participants, e.g., Mansa Musa, King of Mali; Osei Tutu, King of Asante; and Askia Muhammed Toure, King of Songhay.

Question for Group Discussion

   a. When these kings were boys your age, they were usually princes. What kinds of things do you think a prince has to learn if he is to become a great king?

4. **"King for a Day."** In conjunction with this session, construct a king's crown (Appendix B). Explain to participants that a crown sets

a king apart from the rest of the people and was the symbol of his power and authority. Boys should be accorded the honor of wearing the crown during succeeding sessions in recognition of outstanding school achievements.

Session 10: Free to be Me

Goal

The goal of this session is to have participants personalize group activities experienced thus far, both as young Black males and as students.

Methods of Facilitation

1. Play the song, "Just Got to be Myself," by the Voices of East Harlem, which deals with developing a sense of self-identity. Within the context of being young Black males, explore the question "What does it mean to be yourself?"
2. Ask boys, "How does it feel to be a young lion?" and "What have you learned from this group so far?" Record responses on chalkboard. Discuss in greater depth any areas or concepts covered that remain unclear to group members.
3. To further the process of personalizing group experiences, consider again the word "pride." Ask, "What does this word mean to you now?" Ask again, "What kinds of things can you do in school to develop pride in yourself?"

Intended Educational Experiences

1. To have participants learn the importance of individuality.
2. To learn that success in school stems from a sense of pride in oneself.

Sessions 11–13: Heroes
Part 2: African American Men of Distinction

Goal

The goal of these sessions is to have participants examine the boyhoods of famous Black American men in order to gain a greater appreciation for and understanding of the foundation for their accomplishments.

Methods of Facilitation

1. Have participants read aloud the poem, "I, Too, Sing America," by Langston Hughes (Appendix A). This poem is a young Black boy's strong declaration that he will prevail against segregation and take his rightful place in American society. Discuss the meaning of the poem for Black boys today.
2. Read or have participants read brief biographic information focusing on the boyhoods of famous Black Americans such as Louis Armstrong, Arthur Ashe, Guy Bluford, Ralph Bunche, George Washington Carver, Frederick Douglass, W. E. B. DuBois, Alex Haley, Langston Hughes, Jesse Jackson, Martin Luther King, Jr., Thurgood Marshall, Jesse Owens, Jackie Robinson, Booker T. Washington, and Malcolm X.

Questions for Group Discussion

   a. What happened to these men when they were boys that helped to make them famous Americans?
   b. How were their boyhoods like yours?
   c. How were their boyhoods different from yours?
   d. What can you learn about "pride" from these boyhoods?

3. Show excerpts of the Gordon Parks film, "The Learning Tree." This is an autobiographical film directed by a famous Black photographer which traces a year in the life of a young boy. During this year, he learns about love, fear, racial injustice, and his own capacity for honor. Discuss with the participants the differences and similarities between their lives and the life of the young boy in the film.

Intended Learning Experiences

1. To have participants learn about the importance of Black males in American history and culture.
2. To have participants gain an appreciation for the universality of boyhood experiences.
3. To have participants gain a greater understanding of the dynamics of school success.
4. To have participants gain a greater understanding of the relationship between early educational success and achievement in later life.

■

Sessions 14 and 15: Heroes

Part 3: African American Men
of Distinction (Continued)

Goals

The goals of these sessions are: (1) to make participants aware of occupations of contemporary Black men and (2) to impress upon them the important role education plays in obtaining a place in the world of work.

Methods of Facilitation

1. Do a variation of the "On Being Black" exercise (Appendix B). Prepare a questionnaire about Black men in various occupational roles, e.g.:

Do you know a Black man who is an auto mechanic?	Y	N
Do you know a Black man who is a dentist?	Y	N
Do you know a Black man who is a plumber?	Y	N
Do you know a Black man who is a teacher?	Y	N
Do you know a Black man who is a pilot?	Y	N
Do you know a Black man who is a custodian?	Y	N
Do you know a Black man who is a basketball player?	Y	N
Do you know a Black man who is a doctor?	Y	N
Do you know a Black man who is a musician?	Y	N

2. Have participants complete the questionnaire. When finished, total the number of people who know men in each category. Discuss the following questions: When these men were your age, do you think they were good students in school? Why?
3. List the following school subjects on the board: Reading, Math, Language Arts, Spelling, Science, Art, Music, and Social Studies. Review each subject and have participants consider what subjects one would have to be good at to be a success in the listed occupations.
4. Play the "rap" recording, "Knowledge is King,"* by Kool Moe Dee. Discuss what is meant by the term "knowledge is king."

Intended Learning Experiences

1. To have participants learn about the importance of Black males in the contemporary American workforce.
2. To have participants gain a greater understanding of the dynamics of school success.
3. To have participants gain a greater understanding of early educational success to future occupational success.

*Cautionary note: While "rap," as an art form, has its roots in the oral tradition of African/African American people, caution is suggested when using it in empowerment programs. The lyrics of many rap recordings contain language that may not be suitable for young children.

———————■———————

Sessions 16 and 17: Eyes on the Prize

Goal

The goal of this session is to have participants synthesize their learning and experiences from the program into personal action plans.

Methods of Facilitation

1. Play the "rap" recording, "Keep Your Eyes on the Prize," by Young MC. Discuss with the participants the meaning of "keeping your eyes

on the prize." To focus on the notion of school success ask, "What 'prize' should you have your eye on in school?"

2. Ask, "How are you going to win your prize?" On the board, place the following:

Winning the Prize

I am a young lion. I have pride in myself. I will keep my eyes on the prize and do well in school. I will be a success.

*When I am in school I will _____.
*When I am at home I will _____.

Have the participants fill in the blanks with the things they must do, both at home and in school, to succeed academically and socially.

3. Have each participant develop a personal action plan by filling out an individual sheet with his ideas for winning the prize. Have both the boy and his role model/mentor sign the sheet. Encourage them to put it up in a prominent place at home. Share a copy with participants' teachers and parents.
4. Ask each participant to share with the group why he feels that he will "win the prize" and be a success in school.
5. As a final activity, have the group attempt to compose their own "rap" about academic success.

Intended Educational Experience

To have participants learn that academic and social success requires personal commitment and action.

———————————————■———————————————

Session 18: Young Lions—Black and Proud

Goal

The goal of this session is to terminate the group by reinforcing and personalizing activities and experiences.

Methods of Facilitation

1. Note that this will be the last gathering of the pride. Play the recording, "Say It Loud (I'm Black and I'm Proud)," by James Brown. Consider again the word "pride." Ask, "What does this word mean to you now?" Ask again, "What kinds of things can you do in school to develop pride in yourself?"

2. Ask boys, "Now that we have come to the last session, how does it feel to be a young lion?", "How are you like a lion?", and "What have you learned from this group?" Record responses on chalkboard.

3. Place the term, "Pride of Lions," with the suggested accompanying words on the board in the following manner:

P roud		**L** eaders
R espectful		**I** ndustrious
I nitiative	of	**O** bedient
D iligent		**N** ever give up
E xcellence		**S** uccessful

Explain the meaning of each word and its importance to a young lion. Duplicate this and give one to each participant. Encourage them to put it up next to their action plan in a prominent place at home.

4. To reinforce the transfer of group experiences to school success, play the recording, "Ain't No Stopping Us Now," by McFadden and Whitehead. Discuss the inspirational meaning it brings to the lives of young Black males.

5. Conclude with a small celebration with food and music.

Intended Educational Experiences

1. To help participants culminate the process of increasing their self-esteem.

2. To reinforce the notion of commitment to school success.

3. To enhance the sense of brotherhood between boys and role models/mentors.

———————— ■ ————————

Concluding Program

Goal

To honor participants for completing the program.

Method of Facilitation

Conduct some type of concluding program to celebrate successful completion of the program and to reinforce group experiences. Encourage parents, teachers, and administrators to participate in the group participants' celebration.

Sample Program

WELCOME & AFRICAN MEDITATION ....A ROLE MODEL/MENTOR & BOY
SONG...BLACK NATIONAL ANTHEM
REMARKS ABOUT THE GROUP EXPERIENCE ....A ROLE MODEL/MENTOR
INTRODUCTION OF ROLE MODEL/MENTORS ....BOYS
INTRODUCTION OF BOYS.......................................ROLE MODELS/MENTORS
"REFLECTIONS ON BEING YOUNG LIONS"...BOYS

P	ROUD	**L**	EADERS
R	ESPECTFUL	**I**	NDUSTRIOUS
I	NITIATIVE OF	**O**	BEDIENT
D	ILIGENT	**N**	EVER GIVE UP
E	XCELLENCE	**S**	UCCESSFUL

(GROUP MEMBERS STAND UP AND EXPLAIN TO THE AUDIENCE THE IMPORTANCE OF THESE WORDS TO YOUNG LIONS.)

GROUP MEMBERS THEN RECEIVE CERTIFICATES AND A TOKEN SYMBOLIZING THE COMPLETION OF THE PROGRAM FROM ROLE MODELS/MENTORS. (CERTIFICATES MIGHT HAVE A PICTURE OF A LION ATTACHED TO IT. AN EXCELLENT TOKEN IS A CANDLE, SYMBOLIZING THE LIGHT OF KNOWLEDGE. BOYS SHOULD BE TOLD TO KEEP THE CANDLE IN A SAFE PLACE AND BURN IT ON THE DAY THEY GRADUATE FROM HIGH SCHOOL IN RECOGNITION OF THEIR EDUCATIONAL SUCCESS.)

POETRY READING: "TO A NEGRO BOY GRADUATING"
BY EUGENE T. MALESKA ....ROLE MODEL/MENTOR
CLOSING REMARKS

—————————■—————————

Follow-Up Activities

After the program ends, the participants would benefit from follow-up activities that would serve to reinforce the experience. For example, there should be periodic follow-up sessions with the role models/ mentors. In conjunction with this, the role models/mentors should continue consulting with teachers, administrators, and parents to monitor participants' academic and social progress. Additionally, participants should be encouraged to become involved in leadership activities or given important responsibilities within the school (e.g., serving on the student council, safety patrol, etc.).

Conclusion

Increasingly, words like achievement and motivation are not associated with the "Ronalds" in America's elementary schools. Instead, the contemporary elementary school experience sets the tone for a lifetime of failure and frustration for scores of Black males. If they are to have a chance at academic and career success, Black male youth must have the opportunity to master the basic skills and develop the motivation associated with an elementary school education. The "Young Lions" provides such an opportunity. It offers boys such as Ronald, who are at-risk for educational alienation, the chance to spend quality educational time with adult Black male role models. These role models are men who fully understand and appreciate the dynamics of Black male behavior and personality. The combination of individual tutoring and culturally relevant group guidance, which forms the structure of the program, is designed to empower Black male youth for maximum academic and social success in the all-important elementary school years. Counselors are urged to consider implementing such a program as an integral part of a comprehensive strategy for Black male empowerment.

Suggested Group Resources

Session 1

Pride activities from Appendix B.
Webster's Ninth New Collegiate Dictionary published in 1989 by
Merriam-Webster.

Sessions 3–5

"Bad Times," by Tavares from the album, "Supercharged." Capitol
Records, ST12026.
The poem, "Mother to Son," by Langston Hughes in Appendix A.

Sessions 7–9

"Waaslu" by B. Olatunji from the album, "More Drums of Passion."
Columbia Records, C29307.
A series of posters called "Great Kings of Africa," created by Anheuser-
Busch in 1985. For ordering information call Anheuser-Busch in
St. Louis at (314) 577-2000 and say that you want to order the "Great
Kings of Africa" posters. You will be transferred to a recording with
all of the ordering information.

Session 10

"Just Got to be Myself," by The Voices of East Harlem from the album,
"Can You Feel It." Just Sunshine Records, JSS-3504.

Sessions 11–13

The poem, "I, Too, Sing America," by Langston Hughes in Appendix A.
"The Learning Tree," a film by Gordon Parks produced in Hollywood,
California in 1969 by Warner Brothers/Seven Arts, Inc. Available
from Warner Home Video, 1-800-323-4767.

Sessions 14 and 15

Pride activities from Appendix B.
"Knowledge is King," by Kool Moe Dee from the album "Knowledge is
King." Zomba Recording Corp., 1182-4-J

Sessions 16 and 17

"Keep Your Eye on the Prize," by Young MC, from the album,
"Brainstorm." Capitol Records, C4-96337.

Session 18

"Say It Loud (I'm Black and I'm Proud)," by James Brown, from the
album, "James Brown, 20 All Time Greatest Hits." Polydor Records,
314 511 326-4.
"Ain't No Stopping Us Now," by G. McFadden and J. Whitehead, from
the album, "McFadden & Whitehead." Philadelphia International
Records, J235800.

Concluding Program

The poem, "To a Negro Boy Graduating" by Eugene T. Maleska in
Appendix A.

Black Manhood Training: A Developmental Counseling Program for Adolescent Black Males

Introduction

Malik

Malik is a 13-year-old Black male who is in the seventh grade at an urban junior high school. He lives in an apartment complex in a lower middle (working) class neighborhood with his mother and seven-year-old sister. Malik's parents have been divorced since he was six-years old and he sees his father very infrequently.

Throughout his elementary school years, Malik was an honor roll student. However, since starting junior high school, his grades have dropped dramatically and he expresses no interest in doing well academically. He spends his days at school in the company of a group of seventh and eighth grade boys who are frequently in trouble with school officials.

Malik's mother must constantly take time off from her day job to come to school to meet with officials about Malik's poor academic performance and his problematic behavior. On one occasion, when she meets with Malik's counselor, she expresses her frustrations with her son. She explains that she must work two jobs in order to support her children. Since she is often not home when the children get out of school and on the weekends, she depends on Malik to look after himself and his younger sister. She regrets not having the time to spend with Malik and confesses that talk to her and defies her. She says, "Something has gotten into him. He acts like he's grown."

Malik's mother goes on to say that recently he has been staying out late with his group of friends at the corner basketball court. She is very worried because many of the boys and men who loiter around the basketball court have had run-ins with the police for petty thefts and drug dealing.

This case study represents the contemporary reality of many adolescent Black males. There are several important issues which when considered collectively suggest some major challenges to Malik's development. First, although his mother attempts to provide important developmental support for Malik, her efforts are limited due to the economic realities which compel her to spend a significant amount of time away from home. Related to this is the fact that in her absence she has been forced to entrust household and child care responsibilities to Malik. While still a boy, in many respects Malik has been asked to shoulder a man's responsibilities.

Second, while Malik has distinguished himself as a student in the past, peer group pressure has had a negative influence on his current academic performance. It is apparent that within his peer group academic achievement is not valued, as is often the case in adolescence. Instead, the behavioral norm among Malik's friends appears to be attempting to push the limits of school authority. This type of behavior can have only negative consequences for Malik.

Third, and perhaps most significant, like many adolescent Black boys living in a female headed single-parent household, Malik appears to be making the crucial and often difficult boyhood to manhood transition without the benefit of positive adult male role modeling. While the men at the corner basketball court may provide Malik with role models, the nature of their influence on his development is highly questionable. At a time when he is asking the initial questions of manhood and seeking the right direction, there is no responsible male present to provide Malik with direction.

These issues suggest that Malik, like many of his contemporary adolescent Black male peers, may very well be on a fast track to educational and social failure. Without positive intervention, Malik could end up another negative Black male statistic, lost to the streets.

Given the dynamics of development suggested in Malik's case, school counseling professionals should seek to promote the attitudes and behaviors among adolescent Black males that will empower them to function at optimal psychosocial levels. In order to accomplish this, specific guidance is necessary to foster the awareness, knowledge, and skills of adolescent Black males.

This chapter examines a counseling program designed to promote the transition from boyhood to manhood for adolescent Black males. The original conception of the program was introduced by Lee (1987) as a group counseling experience for Black males in grades 7–12. Since its introduction, it has been adopted by middle and secondary school counselors around the country. While the program was originally conceived to be used in schools, it has been modified for implementation in a variety of settings, including fraternal organizations and community agencies. It has also been effectively implemented as a church-based experience (Lee & Woods, 1989).

The program is a developmental "rites-of-passage" experience that was developed within the context and spirit of a traditional African ritual known as manhood training, popularized by Alex Haley (1976) in his classic saga *Roots*. Haley describes how during this training, adolescent boys in traditional African societies were isolated from their families for an extended period of time and given rigorous physical and mental training considered important in the development of men. This training was conducted by men from the community and had as its purpose the development of the attitudes and skills necessary to assume the responsibilities associated with the masculine role. If a boy successfully completed this training, he was formally acknowledged as a man among his people and accorded the rights and responsibilities of a man.

The program described in this chapter was developed, within the context and spirit of this traditional African custom, as a way to help adolescent Black males assume positive masculine roles. The program is a multi-session developmental group guidance experience. Importantly, it redirects the focus of counseling strategies for adolescent Black males from a negative (reactive) stance to a positive (proactive) one. The program provides the opportunity for counselors to help adolescent Black males develop the attitudes and skills to effectively meet environmental challenges that often lead to problems in the school setting and beyond.

Like the elementary school counseling experience presented in the previous chapter, this program makes use of selected Black art forms and culture-specific curriculum materials as educational aids in the guidance process. With this approach, the program stresses the development of strong Black men through a strengthening of body, mind, and soul. This is accomplished by promoting an understanding and appreciation of the Black man in African and African American history and culture, developing achievement motivation, developing positive and responsible behavior, and modeling positive Black male images.

As with the elementary school program, prior to selecting group participants, counselors should consult with parents and school officials about the nature and purpose of the group. Attempts should be made to insure that group composition is heterogeneous with respect to socio-economic status, academic skill level, and extent of disciplinary involvement. Given the importance of modeling, an adult Black male facilitator is crucial for this experience. When necessary, concerted efforts should be made to include competent Black men from the school or community as group leaders.

The program is described here with major additions and modifications that have been made in its structure as a result of widespread use in schools and related settings. Readers are urged to consider the realities of their own institutional setting in establishing the number of sessions or the duration of the group experience. The program is presented as a guideline and, as such, it is open to additional modification. Its use is limited only by the bounds of individual creativity and imagination.

Black Manhood Training: "Body, Mind and Soul"

Goal of the Program

The goal of this program is to help adolescent Black males develop positive masculine identities through a strengthening of body, mind, and soul. This strengthening is accomplished by promoting an understanding and appreciation of the Black man in history and culture, developing achievement motivation, fostering positive and responsible behavior, and modeling positive Black male images.

---■---

Introductory Sessions

Goal

The goal of these sessions is to have group members become aware of the challenges associated with being Black and male and begin to reflect on the notion of masculinity from a Black perspective.

Methods of Facilitation

1. Play the song, "What's Happening Brother?" by Marvin Gaye. Lead a discussion of what is happening to "brothers" internationally, nationally, and locally—identify global and specific challenges confronting Black males.
2. Lead a general discussion of the focal question of the program: "What is a Strong Black Man?" (i.e., a "Brother?").
3. Explore with the group the images of Black men portrayed in the media (i.e., motion pictures and television).

Have members identify these images as positive or negative. Using a chalkboard, place the names of Black men considered by group members to represent positive images in one column and those considered to represent negative images in another. Have the group members explain their choices and defend their selections as positive or negative.

Questions for Group Discussion

a. What makes a man strong?
b. Who are some strong Black men that you know personally? What makes these men strong?
c. Do you think that you are strong? Why?

Intended Counseling Experiences

1. To have group members become more aware of the challenges facing Black males internationally, nationally, and locally.
2. To have group members begin to critically analyze the image of Black men.
3. To have group members begin to analyze the notion of masculinity and strength within a Black perspective. Play the song, "My Name is Man" from the musical, "Don't Bother Me, I Can't Cope," and introduce the notion that masculinity comes from the strength of **Body, Mind,** and **Soul.** Begin to explore with the group members the notion of becoming a man by strengthening one's body, mind, and soul.

---■---

Sessions Related to the Body

Goal

The goal of these sessions is to promote the concept that a strong Black man develops, protects, and cares for his body, i.e., is physically healthy.

Methods of Facilitation

1. Consult with physical education teachers, coaches, and community recreation leaders to ensure that group members are involved in rigorous exercise or athletic programs. Explore with group members why it is important for strong Black men to be physically fit.
2. Play recordings such as, "The Bottle" and "Angel Dust," by Gil Scott-Heron and explore with group participants Black male health hazards. Use recent data from sources such as the National Urban League, National Center for Health Statistics, and the U.S. Department of Health and Human Services to review the health status of Black men in contemporary America.

Discussion Question:

   Is abuse of your body a sign of strength?

3. Play the recording, "The Dude," by Quincy Jones and discuss grooming and dress habits. Show the group participants pictures of well-groomed Black men taken from popular magazines and ask: "What makes a real 'Dude'?" "In terms of dress habits and grooming, how can you tell when a brother 'has his stuff together'?"
4. Discuss the importance of good nutrition and proper eating habits to a physically healthy Black man.

Intended Counseling Experiences

1. To have group members become aware of the importance of developing and maintaining a strong body through physical exercise.
2. To have group members develop a *wellness mentality* which discourages activities that threaten physical health and well-being.
3. To have group members develop good grooming habits.

Sessions Related to the Mind

Goal

The goal of these sessions is to promote the concept that a strong Black man develops and uses his mind to its fullest capacity by fostering the development of the attitude and skills necessary for optimal academic achievement.

Methods of Facilitation

1. To stress the historical importance of academic achievement to Black men, show excerpts from the Public Broadcasting System television series, "Eyes on the Prize," which chronicles the American Civil Rights Movement. Two excerpts of note are James Merideth's attempt to integrate the University of Mississippi in the 1960s and the efforts of Black students to enter Central High School in Little Rock, Arkansas in the 1950s. In addition, through biographic materials, examine the struggles of historical Black male figures (e.g., Frederick Douglass) to get an education. After viewing the excerpts and reading biographic information, discuss with group members the idea that **strong Black men place a high value on education.**

Discussion Questions:

a. What did you learn from "Eyes on the Prize" about strong Black men and education?
b. What lessons can you learn from the life and struggles of men such as Frederick Douglass about strength, Black men, and education?

2. Conduct **motivation sessions** to facilitate the development of positive attitudes toward academic achievement. Develop group guidance activities focusing on inherent Black male potential that incorporate **historical and contemporary** references to the educational experiences of Black males. Expose the group members to both historical and contemporary "Respected Elders," who can speak to them about the importance of education to Black male survival.

a. **Respected Historical Elders.** Have group members explore the **educational contributions** of Black men such as:
   - George Washington Carver
   - W. E. B. DuBois
   - Booker T. Washington
   - Paul Robeson
   - Benjamin Mays
   - Martin Luther King, Jr.

b. **Respected Contemporary Elders.** Invite Black men from various sectors of the community to come to group sessions and share their educational histories with the participants. These might include:
   - Student-athletes from local colleges
   - Professional athletes who have succeeded athletically *and* academically
   - Undergraduate and graduate students from local colleges
   - Men from various sectors of the community who have successfully "made it"

3. Promote "Scholastic Male-bonding" among group members. Develop an **academic support network** within the group, the purpose of which is to have group members draw on each other's scholastic strengths in a collective effort to develop academic skills and competencies. Have members establish **group academic goals** and develop strategies for meeting them.

4. Coordinate tutorial help for group members, as needed.

5. Coordinate the development of skills in the following areas: academic planning, study skills, time management, testwiseness.

   Questions for Group Discussion:

   a. Is education strength?
   b. Why is it important for a **strong** Black man to be an **educated** man?

Intended Counseling Experiences

1. To have group members become aware of the importance of developing and maintaining a strong mind.
2. To have group members learn from "respected elders" (both historical and contemporary) about the wisdom of academic achievement and its importance to Black male survival and success.
3. To have group members develop the attitudes and skills necessary for optimal academic achievement.

Sessions Related to the Soul

Goal

The goal of these sessions is to promote the concept that a strong Black man has an indomitable **spirit.** This is accomplished by fostering an understanding and appreciation of the major life roles and responsibilities of the Black man.

Methods of Facilitation

1. Introduce the Black man's historical struggle to survive and prevail by playing the recording,"I Gotta Keep Moving," from the musical, "Don't Bother Me, I Can't Cope," and having the group read the poem, "The Negro Speaks of Rivers," by Langston Hughes (Appendix A).

Discussion Question:

Given the challenges Black men have always had to face, why have they survived?

2. Explore the various life roles that men can assume. Have members choose the names of Black men who fought for Black pride and glory from various life roles. Each group member is to write a research paper on the person(s) whose name he draws. After researching, members present to the group information about this person(s) that they feel represents something about the **soul/spirit** of the person(s) as a Black man. Black art forms may be used in the presentation. Life roles and names might include:

Warriors: Great Kings of Africa, Hannibal, Crispus Attucks, Nat Turner, Buffalo Soldiers, Hell Fighters, Tuskegee Airmen, Benjamin O. Davis, Colin Powell, Ezell Blair, Joseph McNeil, David Richmond, Franklin McCain

Athletes: Joe Louis, Jackie Robinson, Jesse Owens, Muhammad Ali, Paul Robeson, Wendell Scott, Eddie Robinson, Arthur Ashe, Doug Williams

Artists: Henry O. Tanner, Richard Wright, Ralph Ellison, Langston Hughes, James Van Der Zee, Ernie Barnes, Paul Robeson, Sidney Poitier, Arthur Mitchell, Alvin Ailey, Ray Charles, Wynton Marsalis, Duke Ellington, Stevie Wonder, Denzel Washington

Ministers: Adam Clayton Powell, Elijah Muhammad, Malcolm X, Martin Luther King, Howard Thurman, Jesse Jackson, Desmond Tutu

Entrepreneurs: Henry Parks, John Johnson, Edward Gardner, Earl Graves, Asa Spaulding, Berry Gordy

Scientists: Lewis Lattimer, Charles Drew, Daniel Hale Williams, George Washington Carver, Guy Bluford, Ronald McNair, Fred Gregory

Educators: Benjamin Mays, W. E. B. DuBois, Booker T. Washington, Kenneth Clark

Politicians/ Statesmen:	Great Kings of Africa, Ralph Bunche, Tom Bradley, Andy Young, Wilson Goode, Harold Washington, William Gray, Coleman Young, Richard Hatcher, L. Douglas Wilder, David Dinkins, Jesse Jackson, Nelson Mandela
Journalists:	Frederick Douglass, Carl Rowan, Bryant Gumbel, John Johnson, Earl Graves, William Raspberry, Juan Williams, Ed Bradley, Chuck Stone, Alex Haley

3. Explore in depth the role of the Black man as **father** by examining the word **responsibility**. This stresses the notion that strong Black men take responsibility for their children. Play the recording, "Pappa Was a Rolling Stone," by the Temptations and discuss the negative father images in the song.

Questions for Group Discussion:

   a. Does making babies make you a man?
   b. Does fatherhood bring with it responsibilities? If so, what are some of these responsibilities?
   c. Physically, you can now make babies, but are you ready to be fathers?

4. Conduct a discussion of other key words related to the soul/spirit of strong Black men: masculinity, strength, character, giving, caring, sharing, respect, etc.

Questions for Group Discussion:

   a. What do these words mean to you as young Black men?
   b. What do these words mean for your relationships with other people as young Black men (particularly Black women)?

   Have the group read excerpts from the play, "For Colored Girls Who Have Considered Suicide When the Rainbow is Enuf," that focus on male-female relationships and have the members examine these key words.

5. Paste pictures from magazines (e.g., *Ebony, Essence, Jet*) that present varied images of Black men in many life roles on newsprint. Present

these pictures to the group and examine how the **soul/spirit** of the Black man is portrayed in each image.

6. Show the video presentation, "Black, Male, and Successful in America," which was produced by the Alexandria, Virginia Public Schools. This video highlights the development of positive images and life styles for Black males. Initiate a discussion of the following questions related to the video:
   a. What message about the soul or spirit of the Black man do you get from this video?
   b. As a result of watching this video, what kind of things do you need to do to become a successful Black man?
7. Facilitate personal explorations of various life roles among group members by having them discuss answers to the following questions: "Do you see yourself as a _____?" (son, boyfriend, brother, husband, father, uncle, etc.)

Intended Counseling Experiences

1. To have group members gain an appreciation of the indomitable spirit of struggle and survival inherent in the soul of the strong Black man.
2. To have group members gain a sense of responsibility to self and others.
3. To have group members appreciate how "soul power" permeates the life roles of strong and successful Black men.
4. To have each group member gain a new perspective on his own soul as a young Black man.

———————————————— ■ ————————————————

Developing a Plan for Personal Action

Goal

The goal of these sessions is to have participants synthesize important aspects of the group experience and set personal action goals derived from insights gained from the group.

Method of Facilitation

1. Play again the recording, "My Name is Man," from the musical, "Don't Bother Me, I Can't Cope," and initiate a discussion of what the group experience has meant to each participant in terms of new insights into his body, mind, and soul as a young Black man.

   Discussion Questions:

   a. After all that you have experienced, what is a strong Black man? (a "brother?")
   b. After being in this group, what kind of educational plans do you have?
   c. After being in this group, what kind of career plans do you have?

---------------■---------------

Concluding Activities:

The "Test of Worthiness"

Goal

To "test" the body, mind, and soul of group participants to see if each possesses the strength to be proclaimed a man.

Method of Facilitation

1. Group members are given tests of body, mind, and soul, each of which they must "pass." (Note: The tests and the criteria for passing should be demanding, but flexible enough to insure that the majority of the participants will succeed.)

   a. **Test of the Body.** *Example:* Members must run a quarter of a mile on a track in a specified amount of time to prove that their bodies are strong.
   b. **Test of the Mind.** *Example:* Members must complete a 100-problem math test and get a certain percentage correct to prove that their minds are strong.

   c. **Test of the Soul.** *Example:* Members must participate in some responsible activity at school, at home, at church, or in the community to prove that their souls are strong.

Intended Counseling Experience

To have group members culminate the process of developing their awareness, knowledge, and skills as young Black men.

———————————■———————————

Initiation Ceremony

Goal

To proclaim the manhood of group participants.

Method of Facilitation

Conduct some type of manhood initiation or "rites-of-passage" ceremony to celebrate the manhood of the group members and to reinforce group experiences. Encourage parents and key men from the community to participate in the group participants' celebration.

Sample Initiation Ceremony

PROCESSIONAL...MEN AND BOYS

WELCOME AND AFRICAN MEDITATION...............................GROUP LEADER

SONG...BLACK NATIONAL ANTHEM

REMARKS ABOUT THE GROUP EXPERIENCE ....GROUP LEADER

INTRODUCTION OF RESPECTED ELDERS ....A GROUP MEMBER

"REFLECTIONS ON STRONG BLACK MANHOOD" ....RESPECTED ELDERS

   SPEAKER ON THE BODY ....E.G., A PHYSICIAN

   SPEAKER ON THE MIND...E.G., A TEACHER

   SPEAKER ON THE SOUL ....E.G., A MINISTER

INTRODUCTION OF GROUP MEMBERS TO AUDIENCE..............GROUP LEADER

"RITES OF PASSAGE" ....

(Each group member must stand up in front of the audience and state what it means to him to be a strong Black man.)

Group members then receive certificates or some token symbolizing the completion of manhood training from respected elders.

Closing Remarks and African Meditation .... Group Leader
Recessional .... MEN!

Follow-Up Experiences

After the group experience and the initiation into manhood, the participants would benefit from follow-up activities. These would serve to reinforce the experience. Such activities might include:

1. Periodic follow-up sessions with the leader.
2. Field trips to African/African American cultural institutions.
3. Spending time at work with responsible older Black men.
4. Participation in community service projects.
5. Participation in organized group interaction with their Black female counterparts and their male peers from other ethnic groups, as appropriate.
6. Serving as co-leaders for succeeding manhood training groups.

Conclusion

The boyhood to manhood transition is a challenging developmental phenomenon. For adolescent Black males, such as Malik, the challenges associated with this phenomenon are often compounded by the absence of positive role models to point the way to manhood. With no one to model the attitudes, behaviors, and values of successful Black manhood, many adolescent males wander into self-defeating and self-destructive lifestyles.

The spirit and intent of "Black Manhood Training" is to point adolescent Black male youth in the direction of successful manhood. The program makes a concerted effort to involve successful Black men in the academic, career, and personal-social empowerment of adolescent males. Counselors attempting to incorporate such a program as part of a school counseling curriculum must keep in mind that while almost anyone can successfully raise a Black boy to adulthood, only a Black man can teach him how to be a man.

Suggested Resources

Introduction Sessions

"What's Happening Brother?" by Marvin Gaye, from the album, "What's Going on?" Motown Record Corp., HS1876.
"My Name is Man," by A. Wilkerson, from the Broadway cast album "Don't Bother Me I Can't Cope." Polydor Records, PD-6013.

Body

"The Bottle," by Gil Scott-Heron, from the album, "It's Your World." Arista Records, HS-226.
"Angel Dust," by Gil Scott-Heron, from the album, "Secrets." Arista Records, HS-122.
"The Dude," by Quincy Jones, from the album, "The Dude." A&M Records, SP-3721.

Mind

"Eyes on the Prize: America's Civil Rights Years" [videorecording]. Schools and organizations can order this videorecording from: PBS Video, 1320 Braddock Place, Alexandria, Virginia 22314, 1-800-424-7963. The price of this eight-part series is $395. "Eyes on the Prize" is also widely available at public libraries. Generally, the larger the library, the more likely it is that they will have it.

Soul

"I Gotta Keep Moving," by Alex Bradford, from the Broadway cast album, "Don't Bother Me I Can't Cope." Polydor Records, PD-6013.
The poem, "The Negro Speaks of Rivers," by Langston Hughes from Appendix A.

"Pappa Was a Rolling Stone," by The Temptations, from the album, "The Motown Story." Motown Record Corporation, 6048ML5.

"For Colored Girls Who Have Considered Suicide When the Rainbow is Enuf." Play by Ntozake Shange published in 1975 by Macmillan. Available in bookstores for $5.95.

"Black, Male and Successful in America." Videotape, 14 minutes long, made by the Alexandria, Virginia Public Schools. Available from the American Association for Counseling and Development (AACD), 5999 Stevenson Ave., Alexandria, Virginia 22304, 1-800-347-6647. The price is $75 for AACD members and $85 for nonmembers.

"My Name is Man," by A. Wilkerson, from the Broadway cast album, "Don't Bother Me I Can't Cope." Polydor Records, PD-6013.

MODULE 3

Tapping the Power of Respected Elders: Insuring Male Role Modeling for Black Male Youth

School counseling professionals who want to help empower young Black males using models such as those described in Modules 1 and 2, must insure that competent Black men play a major role in the process. This is important for two reasons. First, only a Black man can teach a Black boy how to be a man. By virtue of attaining adult status as Black and male, he alone has the gender and cultural perspective to accurately address the boyhood-to-manhood transition issues of Black boys. While Black women and individuals of both sexes from other ethnic backgrounds can play a significant role in helping to empower young Black males, it is only a Black man who can model the attitudes and behaviors of successful Black manhood.

Second, there is a paucity of Black male educators in American schools. In reviewing ethnic/gender data for school personnel, Patton (1981) concluded that a majority of Black male students can spend an entire career in school and have very little interaction with a Black male teacher, counselor, or administrator until high school. Even then, as a result of the limited number of Black males at the secondary level, that interaction can be limited.

For these reasons, the challenge for many school counselors is to find ways to include Black men in empowerment interventions for Black male youth. Because the presence of Black males as professionals in the school setting may be limited, counselors must be prepared to look beyond the school for nontraditional male educational resources. While the landscape in many Black communities may be dotted with men who are less than desirable role models, there are countless others whose achievements and experiences make them potential respected elders. These men can significantly influence the cognitive and affective development of young Black males (Washington & Lee, 1982). A concerted effort must be made to find them.

This chapter provides guidelines for getting concerned Black men involved in school-based interventions for the empowerment of young Black males. The focus of the chapter is on selecting and preparing committed Black men to facilitate developmental group experiences, such as "The Young Lions" and "Black Manhood Training."

Role Model Presence in Black Communities: Tapping Black Male Resources

It is important that counselors initiate steps to acknowledge the importance of adult Black male influence on the development of Black boys. These steps must include a validation of such influence by incorporating it into the empowerment process. In most Black communities there is a wealth of positive Black male talent inherent in a variety of institutions and agencies that can be exploited in order to promote empowerment initiatives for young boys.

Churches

Contact the ministers of churches in Black communities and enlist their aid in recruiting concerned men from their congregations to serve as volunteers in the school. Most Black churches have organized men's groups, such as the ushers, or the deacon board, that may be willing to volunteer their services for empowerment efforts.

Community Agencies

Approach the directors of community recreation centers and other social service agencies for potential Black male volunteers. In many instances, such agencies have established youth programs that can serve as important supplements to school-based empowerment interventions.

Fraternities and Social/Service Organizations

In recent years, the graduate chapters of Black fraternities, as well as other social/service organizations in Black communities, have begun to actively address issues associated with young males. Contact these organizations to enlist a cadre of committed volunteers.

Black Businesses

Many Black businessmen have begun to express concern about the challenges facing young Black males. Contact Black entrepreneurs and seek their assistance as volunteers. Also, explore with them the possibility of establishing cooperative programs for Black male youth as a part of the empowerment process.

Colleges and Universities

Explore the possibility of recruiting male students from Black cultural and fraternal organizations on local college campuses. Discuss with academic officials at these institutions the possibility of volunteers receiving academic credit for their efforts.

Prior to venturing into the community, counselors may want to assess the possible Black male resources available in their own school settings. While a Black male presence is often limited in schools, it may be possible to recruit the talents of Black male teachers, administrators, and custodians into the empowerment efforts.

Regardless of the recruitment source, men considered as possible respected elders should, at minimum, exhibit the following criteria: (1) concern about the academic and social challenges facing Black male youth, (2) expressed commitment to helping young Black males, (3) insight into being Black and male, (4) demonstrated success in their personal endeavors, (5) a sense of responsibility, and (6) a willingness to grow as Black men.

From Concern to Action: Preparing Black Men to be "Respected Elders"

Before assuming roles as respected elders, it is important that volunteers have the opportunity to increase their awareness, knowledge, and skills in several areas. First, they should have time to reflect on important aspects of Black manhood. Second, they should be provided with an overview of specific empowerment models for Black male youth. Third, they should learn basic information about group process and how to lead a group experience.

The following training program has been developed and used to prepare volunteers to work as respected elders with both "The Young Lions" and "Black Manhood Training" programs.

———————————■———————————

Respected Elders Training Program

Goal of the Program

To increase the awareness and promote the leadership skills of Black men who volunteer to conduct developmental group experiences with Black male youth in the school setting.

Training Schedule and Format

The training should be conducted in a minimum of two sessions, ideally over a weekend to insure maximum participation. The training format consists of experiential group activities, lecture, and demonstration. This experience can be conducted in a variety of settings, including schools, churches, community centers, or private homes.

Number of Participants

The maximum number of participants for the training program is between 10 and 15.

———————————■———————————

Session 1: Friday, 7:00–10:00 p.m.
Reflections on Black Manhood

This first session is devoted to having the participants take part in a group consciousness-raising experience. This experience is a modification of a developmental group program for Black men called "Reflections on the Native Son" (Lee, 1990). It is designed to help the participants raise their level of masculine consciousness. The experience aims to develop a supportive atmosphere that will enable the men to explore thoughts, feelings, and behaviors associated with being Black and male in contemporary American society.

A Black male facilitator is critical for this session. In addition, during this first session, women should be discouraged from either observing or participating in the process. This insures an atmosphere conducive to optimal male bonding and group discussion.

Methods of Facilitation:

1. "Images of Black Men." Prepare a videotape presentation containing images of Black men. Excerpts from the film version of Richard Wright's *Native Son*, excerpts from the Public Broadcasting System television version of Lorraine Hansberry's play, "A Raisin in the Sun," and excerpts from the motion picture "Glory" are useful examples.
2. Divide the participants into small discussion groups and have them discuss their perceptions of the images of Black men in the videotape.
3. In the small groups have the participants discuss the following important questions to consider as Black men:
   - How do you see yourself as a Black man?
   - What is important to you as a Black man?
   - How do you feel about all those negative stereotypes of and reports about Black men? (e.g., Black men are shiftless, Black men treat Black women disrespectfully, Black men don't take fatherhood seriously, Black men are physically aggressive.)
   - How do you feel about the men in your family?
   - What are your feelings about your own father?
   - If you have children, what kind of a father would they say you are?

- If you have a son(s), how do you think he sees you as a father and as a man?
- When you were growing up, who were your heroes/role models?
- Who are your heroes/role models now?
- How do you feel about the women in your family?
- How do you see and what do you feel about women who are lovers/friends?
- What are the stresses and strains in your relationships with these women?
- What are the points of solid and deep agreement between you and women who are lovers/friends?
- What angers you, hurts you, and brings you fulfillment in your relations with the significant women in your life?
- As a Black man, what brings you satisfaction?
- As a Black man, what gives you purpose?
- As a Black man, what role does religion play in your life?
- As a Black man, what makes you fearful?
- As a Black man, what makes you angry?
- At this point in your life, how do you feel about yourself as a Black man?

4. Bring all of the small groups back together and conduct a general discussion of new personal insights gained on Black manhood as result of the session.
5. Conduct a discussion of the concept of "Respected Elder."

Session 2: Saturday, 9:00 a.m.–3:00 p.m.

Part 1: 9:00–11:00 a.m.

Conduct an overview of empowerment model(s), e.g., "The Young Lions" or "Black Manhood Training." Explain goals, methods of facilitation, and intended outcomes of model(s).

Part 2: 11:00 a.m.–1:00 p.m.

Provide participants with basic information on leading groups:

1. This will *not* be a therapy group. Therapeutic forces will be implicit in the group process, but this experience is *not* group therapy.
2. This will be a group guidance experience for young boys designed to give them an understanding of the Black man in history and culture, to develop in them the motivation and skill to achieve academically in school, to develop positive and responsible behavior among them, and to expose them to positive Black male role models.
3. The group will be a structured group—i.e., the discussion and focus of the group will follow a structured format.
4. As group leaders, your roles will include:
   a. **Initiator**—suggesting ways to consider the topic under discussion
   b. **Clarifier**—making sure points, issues, etc. are clear to all group members
   c. **Elaborator**—expanding on points, ideas, and issues
   d. **Coordinator**—keeping order, clarifying relationships and pulling things together—helping people to talk
   e. **Tester**—making sure the group is on the same wavelength
   f. **Summarizer**—evaluating the group direction and reviewing the material covered
5. In addition, as group leader, you will perform the following tasks:
   a. Encouraging participation by all group members
   b. Mediating group conflicts
   c. Following group consensus on topics, ideas, etc.—never overtly impose your will on the group
   d. Gate-tending—i.e., using both verbal and articulate members as well as reticent members for the good of the group process
6. **Important interpersonal skills for group leaders**—The goal for a group leader is to make each group member feel that he is an individual and a part of the group. The following are interpersonal skills for achieving this goal:
   a. Good non-verbal attending:
      S   face members *squarely* during sessions
      O   use an *open* posture
      L   *lean* in toward members when talking
      E   make appropriate *eye-contact*
      R   appear *relaxed*

    b. Use of minimal encouragers—e.g., shaking head in the affirmative

    c. Respect for group members:
- don't interrupt members unnecessarily
- no value judgements, disapproval or shock
- value group members and try to understand them

    d. Genuineness—e.g., be for real
- communicate without distracting messages
- deal with what is going on in the "here and now"
- be spontaneous and consistent
- be willing to talk about yourself

    e. Empathy and Feelings
- Empathy is being able to "walk a mile in another brother's gym shoes."
- In order to be empathic you have to be able to not only listen but to hear what another person is saying.
- By hearing what groups members are saying, they will hopefully deal with their feelings.
- In your group interactions, always go for the feelings, e.g., "How does that make you feel?" "How do the rest of you feel about that?" "You are feeling _____ because _____."
- Make sure that bad feelings are dealt with either in the group or individually.
- Watch for body language, facial expressions, and voice tone for clues to uneasy feelings among group members.

    f. Summarization—it is important to summarize at the beginning and end of each session.

    g. Commitment and confidentiality

Part 3: 1:00–3:00 p.m.

Allow participants time to synthesize training, ask questions, and plan for program implementation.

1. Discuss personal perceptions of the "Respected Elder" concept.
2. Work out the mechanics of program implementation in schools, e.g., selection of group participants, number of group sessions, scheduling of sessions, length of sessions, number of participants/groups, initiation ceremony, program evaluation, and follow-up activities.
3. Questions and answers.

———————■———————

Follow-up Session
(Conducted at the Conclusion of the
Group Leadership Experience)

After the men have completed their group leadership experience with the boys, a follow-up session should be conducted.
1. Allow the group leaders to analyze the entire experience.
2. Discuss with the participants how being a "Respected Elder" has influenced their perceptions of themselves as Black men.
   a. What have you learned about being Black men as a result of this experience?
   b. As a result of your participation in this experience, what specific changes do you think you will make as a Black man (academically, socially, within the community, etc.)?
   c. What did you think about how the group was run? What is your opinion of specific activities? How would you change the group?
   d. What was the most valuable part of the group for you personally?
   e. Would you like to participate in another group such as this one?

———————■———————

Training Resources

"Native Son," a film based on the book by Richard Wright, produced in Hollywood, California by Diane Silver Productions. Available at local video stores.

"A Raisin in the Sun," a play by Lorraine Hansberry. A 1988 PBS production is available for $69.95 from PBS Video Finders, 1-800-328-7271. A 1961 film starring Sidney Poitier is also available from PBS Video Finders for $14.95, or it can be found at local video stores.

"Glory," a 1990 film produced in Hollywood, California by Tri-Star Pictures. Available at local video stores.

Groups: Process and Practice (4th ed.), a book by Marianne Corey and Gerald Corey, published by Brooks/Cole and available from Wadsworth, Inc. for $31.25, 1-800-354-9706.

The Skilled Helper: A Systematic Approach to Effective Helping (4th ed.), a book by Gerard Egan, published by Brooks/Cole and available from Wadsworth, Inc. for $26.50, 1-800-354-9706.

MODULE 4

Educational Advocacy for Empowering Black Male Students

Anger, frustration, and ultimately, failure represent the educational reality for scores of Black males. The disproportionate number of them who fail or become behaviorally labeled perpetuates a myth that they possess inherent educational deficiencies. Such thinking, however, obscures American educational reality. The educational difficulties confronting Black male youth are often not a function of deficient academic or social skills, but rather the outcome of structural factors. Traditionally, school success has generally been narrowly defined in terms of a White, middle-class female norm (Longstreth, 1974; Patton, 1981). Students whose realities differ from this norm are often required to make important adjustments to ensure a measure of success. If they are unable to do so, they are at considerable risk for mislabeling and negative tracking.

The preponderance of female educators, particularly at the elementary school level, has often created an environment that is not conducive to optimal learning for Black boys (Hale, 1982; Kunjufu, 1986; Washington & Lee, 1982; Patton, 1981). According to Hale (1982), classrooms are generally oriented toward feminine values, and the behaviors encouraged are those that are more natural for girls. While males of other ethnic backgrounds also experience problems in such an environment, Black males experience the greatest difficulty. This is especially the case when these educators have a limited understanding of, or negative preconceived notions about, the dynamics associated with Black male development and culture. Educators frequently have predetermined negative views about Black males and their behavior and academic potential. They see these boys as Black and male; therefore, they expect "double trouble" which can lead to a self-fulfilling prophesy (Washington & Lee, 1982).

In the majority of cases, the responsibility for problematic school functioning comes to rest solely on the ethnic and gender status of the Black male student and its divergence from the educational norm. Little consideration is given to the notion that problematic functioning may in reality be reactive responses by Black male students to a system that tolerates little diversity.

The concerned counselor in such a setting is faced with a unique dilemma. Charged with facilitating Black male student adjustment to the educational system, he or she is confronted with the fact that it is often the system that needs adjustment to the Black male. This is particularly evident when the attitudes and practices of educators suggest a lack of sensitivity to or understanding of the dynamics associated with Black male development.

Role Definition: Counselors as Educational Advocates

The solution to this dilemma lies in a redefinition of the counseling role to account for the fact that problems are not always found in Black male students but often exist in the educational system. Such a redefinition requires an awareness of the systemic barriers to quality education for young Black males and the development of strategies to effectively challenge them.

The role of educational advocate represents such redefinition. The concerned counselor, in such a role, can initiate consultation activities to help his or her fellow educators better understand the dynamics of male development from a Black perspective and make the teaching-learning process more relevant to the realities of young Black males.

A major consultation activity for educational advocates is described in this module. It is a seminar for educators that counselors might consider coordinating with a mandate from school district officials. It has been developed as a comprehensive in-service training experience for teachers and other school personnel on understanding Black male development and promoting academic success among young Black boys.

Background

The seminar is designed as a seven-week training experience. Each session is scheduled for approximately three hours. Consideration should be given to conducting this seminar as an after school (e.g., 4 p.m. to 7 p.m.) professional development activity or as a summer training institute. Plans should be made to award Continuing Education Units, Recertification Points, or College Credit to participants for completing such a seminar.

The teaching of this seminar may need to be a collaborative effort among a school system, local colleges and universities, and community resources. Experts in areas such as Black child and adolescent development, Black psychology, African/African American history and culture, men's issues, multicultural counseling, and curriculum development should be invited to contribute their expertise to the seminar.

Counselors should be prepared to justify to teachers, administrators, school district officials, and the community-at-large the rationale for developing an in-service experience that focuses exclusively on the educational needs of one student group. An important argument for conducting such an experience lies in the data which present the profile of Black males as most at-risk in most school systems. One way to prevent the academic and social problems confronting Black males is to help teachers and other educators develop the awareness, knowledge, and skills to better promote their learning.

While the seminar should be open to all educators, it is highly recommended for teachers of grades 3–4. As noted previously, these have been found to be particularly problematic years in the educational development of Black males.

Professional Development Seminar: Issues in Educating Black Males

Seminar Description

The purpose of this seminar is to provide an overview of the issues and challenges related to the educational development of young Black males in contemporary schools. Emphasis will be placed on strategies for promoting the academic success of Black males. Participants will also gain an appreciation of African/African American culture and its role in promoting the psychosocial development of male youth.

Objectives

1. To raise educator awareness of personal values and biases which may be detrimental to the welfare of Black male students.
2. To raise educator awareness of the developmental issues and challenges facing Black males.
3. To provide historical/statistical/cultural information to raise educator awareness of the challenges confronting Black males.
4. To identify instructional practices which impede academic progress for Black males.
5. To identify instructional practices which enhance academic progress for Black males.

Seminar Content

---■---

Session 1: Introduction and Overview

1. Seminar Introduction—Review of Goals, Objectives, Readings, Requirements, etc.
2. The Black Male in America: A Social/Historical Overview
3. Education and Achievement of Young Black Males: A National and Local Overview
4. "Fourth Grade Failure Syndrome"

---■---

Session 2: Examining Educator Attitudes and Behavior

Experiential Activity 1: Exploring Personal Attitudes Toward Black Males

1. Divide seminar participants into small groups. Have them take a few minutes to reflect upon the following questions and then discuss their answers in the small groups.
   - To what extent do you regularly interact with Black males professionally? Socially?
   - What was your parents' main advice to you about Black males?
   - How would your parents have responded if, while in college, you had invited a Black male home with you for Thanksgiving?
   - How would you respond if your teenage daughter was dating a Black male?
   - How do you think you would respond if your college-age daughter announced plans to marry a Black male?
   - What is the origin or source of most of your views about Black males? What have you ever done to validate your beliefs about Black males? How do your beliefs affect your behavior toward Black males in the classroom?
   - What is the nicest/meanest, most helpful/hurtful thing a Black male ever said or did to you? What did you feel? What did you do?
   - Describe how you feel when you teach or think about teaching young Black males.
   - What personal attributes do you have which enhance your working with Black males in the classroom?
2. Debriefing

Experiential Activity 2: Examining Classroom Behavior Toward Black Males

1. Have seminar participants examine the incidence of discipline in their classrooms and answer the following: Do the Black males in my class receive a disproportionate share of reprimands or negative feedback?

2. Have participants examine other classroom behaviors and answer the following:
   - Do the stereotypes or perceptions I may have acquired about Black boys influence my behavior towards them and expectations of them?
   - Do I expect disciplinary problems from them and behave accordingly?
   - Do I expect low achievement from them and behave accordingly?
   - Is my instructional behavior reactive, rather than proactive when it comes to Black males?
3. Debriefing

■

Session 3: Psychosocial Development

The Psychosocial Development of Black Males: The Childhood and Adolescent Years

■

Session 4: African/African American Male Culture

"Cool Pose" as a Cultural Signature of Young Black Males: Exploring Positive Black Male Attitudes, Values, and Behaviors and their Cultural Origins

■

Session 5: Cognitive Styles: Implications for the Effective Teaching of Black Males

1. Definition of cognitive style
2. Cognitive style and cultural groupings

3. Cognitive style comparisons
4. Cognitive style implications for the teaching of Black males

---

Session 6: Curriculum Content and Methods That Enhance Academic Progress for Black Male Students

1. Integrating the accomplishments of Black men into the existing curriculum structure.
2. Examining curriculum to insure that Black males are included in primary and nonstereotyped roles.
3. Insuring the inclusion of Black males in classroom activities (e.g., tutors, educational assistants, storytellers, "room fathers," and field trip escorts).
4. Encouraging the participation of Black males in parent-teacher associations and other school organizations.
5. The importance of non-educational personnel (e.g., Black male custodians and lunchroom staff) as valid role models/mentors.

Session 7: FORUM—Perspectives on the Education of Young Black Males

A panel of Black men from various social and professional backgrounds will discuss their personal educational experiences and offer their perceptions of the current state of education for young Black males.

Seminar Readings

Required Texts

Gibbs, J. T. (Ed.) (1988). *Young, Black, and male in America: An endangered species*. NY: Auburn House.

Hale, J. (1982). *Black children, their roots, culture, and learning styles*. Provo, UT: Brigham Young University Press.

Required Readings

Anderson, J. A. (1988). Cognitive styles and multicultural populations. *Journal of Teacher Education, 39,* 2–9.

Boykins, W. (1983). The academic performance of Afro-American children. In J. Spence (Ed.), *Achievement and achievement motives*. San Francisco, CA: W. H. Freeman Co.

Cazanave, N. (1981). Black men in America: The quest for manhood. In H. McAdoo (Ed.), *Black families*. Beverly Hills, CA: Sage Publications.

Gaston, J. (1986). The destruction of the young Black male: The impact of popular culture and organized sports. *Journal of Black Studies, 16,* 369–384.

Kunjufu, J. (1985). *Countering the conspiracy to destroy Black boys* (Vol. 1). Chicago: African American Images.

Kunjufu, J. (1986). *Countering the conspiracy to destroy Black boys* (Vol. 2). Chicago: African American Images.

Majors, R. (1986). Cool pose: The proud signature of Black survival. *Changing Men: Issues in Gender, Sex and Politics, 17,* 5–6.

Patton, J. (1981). The Black male's struggle for an education. In L. E. Gary (Ed.), *Black men*. Beverly Hills, CA: Sage Publications.

Staples, R. (1978). Masculinity and race: The dual dilemma of Black men. *Journal of Social Issues, 34,* 169–183.

Taylor, R. L. (1989). Black youth, role models, and the social construction of identity. In R. L. Jones (Ed.), *Black adolescents*. Berkeley, CA: Cobb & Henry Publishers.

Washington, V., & Lee, C. C. (1982). Teaching and counseling Black males in grades K to 8. *Journal of the National Association of Black Social Workers, 13,* 25–29.

Suggested Readings

Brown, C. (1965). *Manchild in the promised land.* NY: Macmillan.
Haley, A., & Malcom X. (1964). *The autobiography of Malcom X.* NY: Grove Press, Inc.
Wright, R. (1937). *Black boy.* NY: Harper & Row.
Wright, R. (1940). *Native son.* NY: Harper & Row.

Seminar Requirements

1. **Readings:** Required texts and readings.
2. **Participation:** Small group activities and seminar discussion will be an important part of the instruction.
3. **Written Assignments:** Four 300-word essays reacting to any of the required readings. The essays must include the following points:
   a. a brief summary of the author's main points or ideas
   b. your reactions, questions, opinions, etc. regarding the author's ideas from your vantage point as a teacher or possible teacher of young Black males.
4. **Lesson Plan:** A fully developed lesson plan (Goals, Behavioral Objectives, Methods, Materials and Resources, and Evaluation) in a specific content area that incorporates Black male accomplishments and makes allowances for Black male learning styles.

Conclusion

A seminar such as this demonstrates a commitment on the part of a school system to foster maximum educational development for Black males. Counselors acting as educational advocates can be in the forefront of initiating such a consultation activity to help their fellow educators better understand the dynamics of male development from a Black perspective and make the teaching-learning process more relevant to the realities of young Black males.

CHAPTER 5

A Counselor Call to Action: A Comprehensive Approach to Empowering Young Black Males

Introduction

The distressing figures related to the lack of basic competencies, disruptive behavior, and dropout rates for Black male students in America's schools present a major challenge to counseling professionals. Basic to addressing this challenge must be a definitive notion of the counseling role. As the preceding chapters have indicated, school counselors need to develop new perspectives on ways to promote educational empowerment for Black males. It is important that counselors be a major influence in offering solutions to the educational challenges confronting this embattled group of young people. A concerted effort is needed to develop comprehensive counseling strategies that reflect the needs and realities of young Black males. Implicit in such strategies must be the notion that counselors are agents of change, who have the knowledge and skill to translate caring into empowerment initiatives. As this book has suggested, such initiatives necessitate extending programmed intervention beyond the Black male student into the school and community.

This final chapter reviews specific roles and functions considered critical for improving the

...school counselors need to develop new perspectives on ways to promote educational empowerment for Black males.

...counselors are agents of change, who have the knowledge and skill to translate caring into empowerment initiatives.

quality of education for Black male students. In addition, important counselor functions related to the concerns of school personnel and the educational commitment of the Black community are presented. These roles and functions form the basis for a comprehensive school-based Black male empowerment initiative.

The Counselor and the Black Male Student

Concerned counselors must help empower young Black males to develop the attitudes, behaviors, and skills for success in school and the demanding world beyond.

The achievement, aspirations, and pride of many Black males have been seriously stifled in the school setting. Concerned counselors must help empower young Black males to develop the attitudes, behaviors, and skills for success in school and the demanding world beyond. Counselors, therefore, must assume the role of student development facilitator and engage in functions that transcend the traditional boundaries of educational helping. Specific empowerment strategies are needed for heightening awareness, expanding skills, and maximizing options on the part of Black male youth.

Personal-Social Empowerment

...it is only when Black males accept themselves and their realities with a sense of pride that tangible educational gains are possible.

Developing a positive self-identity in young Black males is a primary empowerment function for student development facilitators. Such a task is underscored by the failure identity fostered in scores of Black males through educational experiences that are often insensitive to the dynamics of their psychosocial development or their cultural realities. Such a function must serve as the basis for all others; for it is only when Black males accept themselves and their realities with a sense of pride that tangible educational gains are possible. The interventions described in Modules 1 and 2 for example, represent empowerment models whose fundamental goal is to promote positive self-identity among participants.

Academic Empowerment

Consulting with teachers to foster the development of motivation and skills for academic achievement among Black male students represents the major counselor role in the realm of academic empowerment. Concerned counselors need to work with teachers to insure that the teaching-learning process maximizes the potential of Black male youth. This might entail consulting with teachers to provide such things as tutorial programs, academic planning initiatives, or study skills seminars. In addition, counselors should insure that they play an active role in any school system initiatives which might include the implementation of controversial educational programs, such as recent proposals for segregated classes or schools for Black males.

Concerned counselors need to work with teachers to insure that the teaching-learning process maximizes the potential of Black male youth.

Career Development

The world of work for many Black males has been landscaped with unfulfilled dreams, wasted potential, dashed hopes, and economic struggle. Given this history, the issue of career interest and choice becomes a complex dimension in the development of Black male youth. The committed counselor, therefore, must consider the social pressures on Black male career development and restructure traditional career guidance accordingly. Career empowerment for Black male students should include disseminating information on and encouraging the exploration of nonstereotyped jobs and careers. Importantly, career development interventions should provide adult Black males as career role models and mentors who can explain their perceptions and experiences in the world of work.

The world of work for many Black males has been landscaped with unfulfilled dreams, wasted potential, dashed hopes, and economic struggle.

The Counselor and the Educational System

In working with the educational system to empower young Black males, counselors must assume the role of educational advocate. Such professionals understand that educational problems do not always start with Black male students but often exist in the system. Educational advocacy begins with a knowledge of systemic barriers to quality education for Black male youth and the development of skills to effectively challenge them.

Educational advocacy begins with a knowledge of systemic barriers to quality education for Black male youth and the development of skills to effectively challenge them.

Educational advocates consult with teachers, administrators, and related professionals to identify alienating factors in attitudes, behaviors, or policies concerning Black male students. They also actively participate in the coordination of professional development experiences for educators on ways to incorporate the Black male cultural experience into the total curriculum. The curriculum guide presented in Module 4 is an example of such educational advocacy.

The Counselor and the Black Community

The Black male brings to the school experience cultural attitudes, behaviors, and values fostered in the institutions within his community. However, cultural insensitivity in the educational system often invalidates the cultural realities of these Black institutions. Because of this, valid representatives of these institutions are often excluded from serious consideration in the educational empowerment of Black males.

...cultural insensitivity in the educational system often invalidates the cultural realities of these Black institutions.

Counselors can play an active role in bridging this gap by serving as a liaison between the school and the Black community.

They can work to promote the development and incorporation of family and community resources into the educational empowerment process for Black male youth. This might involve helping parents to better understand standardized testing, to conduct constructive conferences with teachers, or to assess aspects of the curriculum. Thus, counselors would be promoting active involvement by parents in the education of their sons. Other counselor efforts might also include coordinating paraprofessional development programs, such as the one described in Module 3 to involve responsible, committed, and mature Black men from the community in empowerment interventions for boys.

Other counselor efforts might also include coordinating paraprofessional development programs....

The Challenge

The future status of Black men in America depends, in large measure, on the ability of educators to improve the academic success of Black male youth. Counselors can play a proactive role in empowering Black males for maximum educational achievement and productive lives. Accomplishing this, however, will require a comprehensive and systematic approach to the issues of educational empowerment. Such an approach implies a rejection of many long-standing traditions characteristic of the school counseling profession. In assuming the roles and attempting to implement the functions considered in this chapter, counselors can no longer commit themselves solely to the task of facilitating Black male adjustment to the educational system. Empowerment for Black male students will be enhanced by planning strategically and including support from school personnel, revising curriculum to reflect Black male realities, and enlisting the cultural expertise of representatives from the Black community. These things should be done with the aim of having Black males persist and succeed in the educational system.

Counseling professionals who understand the crisis and the challenges associated with being Black and male in America constitute a potent force for

The future status of Black men in America depends, in large measure, on the ability of educators to improve the academic success of Black male youth.

Empowerment for Black male students will be enhanced by planning strategically...and enlisting the cultural expertise of representatives from the Black community.

making educational empowerment for Black male youth a reality. They stand ready to answer the call to action. The Ronalds and Maliks in our school systems are waiting for such action. They deserve no less.

REFERENCES

Allen, W. R. (1981). Moms, dads, and boys: Race and sex differences in the socialization of male children. In L. E. Gary (Ed.), *Black men* (pp. 99–114). Beverly Hills, CA: Sage Publications.

Barnes, E. J. (1991). The Black community as the source of positive self-concept for Black children: A theoretical perspective. In R. L. Jones (Ed.), *Black psychology* (3rd. ed., pp. 667–692). Berkeley, CA: Cobb & Henry.

Clark, K. B., & Clark, M. P. (1947). Racial identification and preference in Negro children. In T. M. Newcomb & E. L. Hartley (Eds.), *Readings in socio-psychology* (pp. 169–178). New York: Holt, Rinehart and Winston.

Committee to Study the Status of the Black Male in the New Orleans Public Schools. (1988). *Educating Black male youth: A moral and civic imperative. An introspective look at Black male students in the New Orleans Public Schools.* New Orleans, LA: Orleans Parish School Board. (ERIC Document Reproduction Service No. ED 303 546)

Congress of the United States. (1991). *The economic status of African Americans: Hearing before the subcommittee on investment, jobs, and prices of the joint economic committee.* Washington, DC: U.S. Government Printing Office.

Cordes, C. (1985, January). At risk in America: Black males face high odds in a hostile society. *APA Monitor,* pp. 9, 10, 11, 27.

Cross. A. (1974). The Black experience: Its importance in the treatment of Black clients. *Child Welfare, 52,* 158–166.

Erikson, E. (1950). *Childhood and society.* New York: Norton.

Freiberg, P. (1991, May). Separate classes for Black males? *The APA Monitor,* pp. 1, 47.

Gary, L. W. (Ed.). (1981). *Black men.* Beverly Hills, CA: Sage Publications.

Gibbs, J. T. (1984). Black adolescents and youth: An endangered species. *American Journal of Orthopsychiatry, 54,* 6–21.

Gibbs, J. T. (1988a). Young Black males in America: Endangered, embittered, and embattled. In J. T. Gibbs (Ed.), *Young, Black and male in America: An endangered species* (pp. 1–36). New York: Auburn House.

Gibbs, J. T. (Ed.). (1988b). *Young, Black, and male in America: An endangered species.* New York: Auburn House.

Goldberg, H. (1976). *The hazards of being male: Surviving the myth of masculine privilege.* New York: New American Library.

Grier, W. H., & Cobbs, P. M. (1968). *Black rage.* New York: Basic Books.

Hale, J. E. (1982). *Black children: Their roots, culture, and learning styles.* Provo, UT: Brigham Young University Press.

Haley, A. (1976). *Roots.* Garden City, NY: Doubleday.

Harper, F. (1973). What counselors must know about the social sciences of Black Americans. *Journal of Negro Education, 42,* 109–116.

Havighurst, R. J. (1972). *Developmental tasks and education* (3rd ed.). New York: McKay.

Hernton, C. (1965). *Sex and racism in America.* New York: Grove.

Hilliard, A. G. (1985). A framework for focused counseling on the African American man. *Journal of Non-White Concerns in Personnel and Guidance, 13,* 72–78.

House of Representatives. (1989). *Barriers and opportunities for America's young Black men* (Hearing before the Select Committee on Children, Youth, and Families). Washington, DC: U.S. Government Printing Office. (ERIC Document Reproduction Service No. ED 314 526)

House of Representatives. (1990). *Hearing on the office of educational research and improvement* (Hearing before the Subcommittee on Select Education of the Committee on Education and Labor). Washington, DC: U.S. Government Printing Office.

House of Representatives. (1991). *Economic status of African Americans* (Hearing before the Subcommittee on Investment, Jobs and Prices of the Joint Economic Comittee.) Washington, DC: U.S. Government Printing Office.

Jones, K. M. (1986). Black male in jeopardy. *Crisis, 93,* 16–21, 44–45.

Kohlberg, L. (1966). Moral education in the schools: A developmental view. *School Review, 74,* 1–30.

Kunjufu, J. (1984). *Developing positive self-images and discipline in Black children.* Chicago: African American Images.

Kunjufu, J. (1986). *Countering the conspiracy to destroy Black boys* (Vol. 2). Chicago: African American Images.

Leavy, W. (1983, August). Is the Black male an endangered species? *Ebony,* pp. 40–49.

Lee, C. C. (1987). Black manhood training: Group counseling for male Blacks in grades 7–12. *Journal for Specialists in Group Work, 12,* 18–25.

Lee, C. C. (1989). Counseling Black adolescents: Critical roles and functions for counseling professionals. In R. L. Jones (Ed.), *Black adolescents* (pp. 298–308). Berkeley, CA: Cobb & Henry.

Lee, C. C. (1990). Black male development: Counseling the "native son." In D. Moore &

F. Leafgren (Eds.), *Problem-solving strategies and interventions for men in conflict* (pp. 125–137). Alexandria, VA: AACD Press.

Lee, C. C., & Lindsey, C. R. (1985). Black consciousness development: A group counseling model for Black elementary school students. *Elementary School Guidance and Counseling, 19,* 228–236.

Lee, C. C., & Woods, C. W. (1989). *Black manhood training: Body, mind, and soul. A church-based group counseling experience for adolescent Black males.* Unpublished manuscript.

Longstreth, L. E. (1974). *Psychological development of the child* (2nd ed.). New York: New York Press.

Majors, R. (1986). Cool pose: The proud signature of Black survival. *Changing Men: Issues in Gender, Sex, and Politics, 17,* 5–6.

McGhee, J. D. (1984). *Running the gauntlet: Black men in America.* New York: National Urban League.

Morgan, H. (1980). How schools fail Black children. *Social Policy, 10,* 49–54.

Myers, H. F., & King, L. M. (1980). Youth of the Black underclass: Urban stress and mental health. *Fanon Center Journal, 1,* 1–27.

National Black Child Development Institute. (1990). *The status of African American children: Twentieth anniversary report, 1970–1990.* Washington, DC: Author.

Nobles, W. (1980). African philosophy: Foundations for a Black psychology. In R. L. Jones (Ed.), *Black psychology* (2nd ed., pp. 23–36). New York: Harper & Row.

Pasteur, A. B., & Toldson, I. L. (1982). *Roots of soul: The psychology of Black expressiveness.* Garden City, NY: Anchor Press/Doubleday.

Patton, J. M. (1981). The Black male's struggle for an education. In L. E. Gary (Ed.), *Black men* (pp. 199–214). Beverly Hills, CA: Sage Publications.

Piaget, J. (1970). *Science of education and the psychology of the child.* New York: Onion Press.

Pleck, J. H., & Sawyer, J. (Eds.). (1974). *Men and masculinity.* Englewood Cliffs, NJ: Prentice-Hall.

Reed, R. J. (1988). Education and achievement of young Black males. In J. T. Gibbs (Ed.), *Young, Black, and male in America: An endangered species* (pp. 37–96). New York: Auburn House.

Staples, R. (1978). Masculinity and race: The dual dilemma of Black men. *Journal of Social Issues, 34,* 169–183.

Staples, R. (1983). *Black masculinity: The Black male's role in American society.* San Francisco: Black Scholar Press.

Taylor, R. L. (1977). Socialization to the Black male role. In D. Y. Wilkinson & R. L. Taylor (Eds.), *The Black male in America: Perspectives on his status in contemporary society* (pp. 1–6). Chicago: Nelson-Hall.

Thomas, A., & Sillen, S. (1972). *Racism & psychiatry.* Secaucus, NJ: The Citadel Press.

Washington, V., & Lee, C. C. (1982). Teaching and counseling Black males in grades K to 8. *Journal of the National Association of Black Social Workers, 13,* 25–29.

White, J. L. (1970). Toward a Black psychology. *Ebony, 25,* pp. 44–45, 48–50, 52.

White, J. L., & Johnson, J. A. (1980). Awareness, pride, and identity: A positive educational strategy for Black youth. In R. L. Jones (Ed.), *Black psychology* (2nd ed.), pp. 273–280. New York: Harper & Row.

Wilkinson, D. Y., & Taylor, R. L. (1977). *The Black male in America: Perspectives on his status in contemporary society.* Chicago: Nelson-Hall.

Wilson, A. N. (1987). *The developmental psychology of the Black child.* New York: Africana Research Publications.

APPENDIX A

Four Poems

I, Too

I, too, sing America.

I am the darker brother.
They send me to eat in the kitchen
When company comes,
But I laugh,
And eat well,
And grow strong.

Tomorrow,
I'll be at the table
When company comes.
Nobody'll dare
Say to me,
"Eat in the kitchen,"
Then.

Besides,
They'll see how beautiful I am
And be ashamed—

I, too, am America.

—By Langston Hughes

Reprinted with permission of Alfred A. Knopf, New York.

The Negro Speaks of Rivers

(To W. E. B. DuBois)

I've known rivers:
I've known rivers ancient as the world and older than the flow of human
    blood in human veins.
My soul has grown deep like the rivers.

I bathed in the Euphrates when dawns were young.
I built my hut near the Congo and it lulled me to sleep.
I looked upon the Nile and raised the pyramids above it.
I heard the singing of the Mississippi when Abe Lincoln went down to New
    Orleans, and I've seen its muddy bosom turn all golden in the sunset.

I've known rivers:
Ancient, dusky rivers.

My soul has grown deep like the rivers.

—By Langston Hughes

Mother to Son

Well, son, I'll tell you:
Life for me ain't been no crystal stair.
It's had tacks in it,
And splinters,
And boards torn up,
And places with no carpet on the floor—
Bare.
But all the time
I'se been a-climbin' on,
And reachin' landin's,
And turnin' corners,
And sometimes goin' in the dark
Where there ain't been no light.
So boy, don't you turn back.
Don't you set down on the steps
'Cause you finds it's kinder hard.
Don't you fall now—
For I'se still goin', honey,
I'se still climbin',
And life for me ain't been no crystal stair.

—By Langston Hughes

Reprinted with permission of Alfred A. Knopf, New York.

To a Negro Boy Graduating

Be wary, lad; the road up which you go
Is long and steeper than you dare to think.
And since you leave in darkness, lad, be slow—
Test every spring before you bend to drink;
Learn now the rose may hide a hundred scars,
The welcome breeze may herald storms ahead.
And though your eyes would trace the course of stars
Or gaze on gray horizons growing red,
Let caution rule your step that you may see
The gaping pit, the waiting bog, the wall
Of white which you must scale. Go carefully
And hopefully; but if somewhere you sink or fall,
Remember where you walked you smoothed the way
That those who follow may discover day.

—*By Eugene T. Maleska*

Reprinted with permission of Doubleday, New York.

APPENDIX B

Three Pride Activities

What is Pride? (Grades 6–8)

Purpose: To help develop self-concept.

Materials: Pencil and paper.

Introduction: Write the meaning for the word "pride" on the board. Have someone read the meaning aloud. Ask the question, "How many of you have pride?" Have the students make a list of things in which they have pride.

Variation: Younger children could draw pictures of things in which they have pride. Older children could discuss how and why men have fought for pride of self and country.

Correlation: This activity could be integrated with language arts activities, emphasizing correct spelling and writing skills.

King's Crown (Grades K–4)

Purpose: To increase student's awareness of African History.

Materials: Construction paper, stapler, pencil, scissors, and a ruler.

Introduction: Africa had many great kings and queens. Probably one of the most outstanding kings was the Ashanti king. One queen who will always be remembered is Cleopatra, the beautiful queen of Egypt. Many of the kings and queens wore beautiful crowns to symbolize their rank. The crowns we are going to make will not be made of diamonds or gold like the African crowns, but ours will have a close resemblance.

Directions: Cut regular size construction paper into halves. Have the children draw an outline of the top of the crown. Cut out the pattern. Staple the two ends together to fit the student's head.

Variation: The teacher could bring in a short report on famous African kings or queens. She could bring in pictures from encyclopedias and resource books related to this subject.

On Being Black (Grades 1–4)

Purpose: To make students aware of occupations that many Black people have.

Materials: Paper, pencils.

Introduction: Today we are going to talk about what it means to be Black in the various occupational fields. There is a list of questions on the board for you to copy.

Questions: (listed on the board)

		Yes	*No*
1.	Do you know a Black baseball player?	☐	☐
2.	Do you know a Black doctor?	☐	☐
3.	Do you know a Black lawyer?	☐	☐
4.	Do you know a Black carpenter?	☐	☐
5.	To you know a Black actor?	☐	☐
6.	Do you know a Black dentist?	☐	☐

Instructions: Put a check in either the *Yes* or *No* box for each question. After the children have finished checking each question, discuss the following: How many people know a Black doctor, lawyer, etc.? Total the number of people who know someone in each category. How many people would like to be working in one of these occupations and why? Do you think that color makes a difference in some of these occupations? Why?

Variation: Children might enjoy doing research to discover unusual professions in which Black people are involved and report back to the class.

Correlation: A lesson in the use of resource materials (how to locate specific types of information) would be useful for this activity.

These three activities are from a book called *Pride: A Handbook of Black Studies Techniques for the Classroom Teacher* by Clifford D. Watson. The book at present is out of print. It was published in 1971 by Educational Service, Inc. in Stevensville, Michigan.